Heavenly Vegan
DALS & CURRIES

EXCITING NEW DISHES

From an Indian Girl's Kitchen Abroad

RAKHEE YADAV

Creator of boxofspice

PAGE STREET
PUBLISHING CO.

PAGE STREET
PUBLISHING CO.

First published in 2019 by

Page Street Publishing Co.

27 Congress Street, Suite 105

Salem, MA 01970

www.pagestreetpublishing.com

Distributed by Macmillan, sales in Canada by The Canadian Manda Group.

23   22   21   20   19   1   2   3   4   5

ISBN-13: 978-1-62414-729-6

ISBN-10: 1-62414-729-1

Library of Congress Control Number: 2018955650

Cover and book design by Meg Baskis for Page Street Publishing Co.

Photography and styling by Rakhee Yadav

Printed and bound in China

This book is dedicated to the world we live in, the world
I leave behind for my daughter.

It is an endeavor to strive for respect for our environment,
to eating consciously and always in moderation.

It is dedicated to my holistic and humble upbringing that made this
thought process survive within me and to the woman, my mother,
who taught me to be forever modest and without excess.

INTRODUCTION

I was raised purely on plant-based foods, and India's abundance of plant life ensured a diversified meal plan. We never missed meat nor did our health suffer as a result of it. In fact, I attribute my good health to eating purely plant-based foods. Buying food seasonally and locally also made sure that our wallet didn't suffer and neither did the flavors of our meals. It is my mother's love for simple, wholesome and delicious food—alongside her philosophy for minimum waste—that resonates in my cooking approach to this day.

The recipes here were created out of an intense love for plant-based foods, and I hope to show you how exciting vegan food can be and what a plethora of choices you have. Indian food—besides being easy to cook—is extremely diverse and for the most part, naturally vegan. These recipes are sometimes quirky with flavors you may never think to combine and sometimes as familiar as your mother's cooking.

Growing up, dals and curries were my absolute favorite part of the meal and have a special place in my heart. Dals are known as "poor man's food" in India because of how cheap the ingredients are and how easy they are to cook. Dals—chickpeas, beans and lentils—have endless possibilities and can easily be combined into curries alongside vegetables. They also have a long list of health benefits, and no one makes them quite like the Indians do.

Eaten as you would soups in the West, dals make a great meal by themselves or can be eaten with rice, rotis or naan bread, like the Indians would. At home in India or abroad, no meal is complete without a dal or curry. Dals may be humble and unassuming, but they are the ultimate comfort food. The dals and the deeply soul-satisfying curries in this book combine age-old flavors with new international twists to great success—some recipes are downright addictive.

I create all of my recipes in my little kitchen—my favorite place in the house—in The Netherlands. Here I am surrounded by the beloved flavors and exotic fragrances of my favorite hand-ground masalas and the wisps and threads of the memories they hold. Hidden in the fragrance of these familiar scents are stories of my childhood and my family, which are woven into this book.

Those familiar aromas and the vision of my mother cooking effortlessly are my inspiration for everything I do and every recipe I develop. Everyday spices such as turmeric and cumin that are so popular today were used frequently back then and are still a big part of my cooking, whether fusion or traditional. This book is a direct reflection of the traditional dishes I grew up on, combined with updated dishes inspired by my travels. The result, in my opinion, is a dramatic bang of flavors, colors and textures that you are going to love.

I hope this book and its contents will inspire you to be creative with your food, mixing and combining different elements from different chapters to make your own inventions. I hope this book also persuades you to minimize waste by substituting one ingredient in a recipe with another that you already may have in your house. If you are a new vegan, this book will show you how versatile and appetizing vegan food is, and if you have always been a plant-based eater like me, I hope this book may entice you into trying something new.

Quick & Easy
MEATLESS WONDERS

We all know that cooking food lovingly and slowly can bring out flavor like nothing else. And there is no food that confirms and demonstrates this more than Indian food. We also see this with the women in India, who spend most of their days in the kitchen, slowly stirring their pots with a huge measure of masala and love thrown in.

It is, however, possible to do quick Indian meals. My mom was a genius at it.

This chapter shows you how an Indian dish with all its flavor and amazing exotic spices is attainable in an hour or less. Perfect for those busy weeknights when all you want is a delicious dish on your lap to savor as you relax after a hard day's work.

In India, korma is usually a dish with a thick sauce made with yogurt and a variety of vegetables or meat wrapped in its creamy flavors. In my version, I removed the creamy aspect and roasted the vegetables in the korma spices. I also added a spicy chutney, homemade Indian bread and sweet nectarines, which makes this meal not only versatile but also super healthy.

ROASTED VEGETABLES & MARROWFAT PEAS IN KORMA SPICES *with* SRIRACHA MINT CHUTNEY

Serves 4

ROASTED KORMA SPICE MIX
2 tbsp (10 g) coriander seeds
2 green cardamom pods
1 small black cardamom pod
½" (13-mm) cinnamon stick
3–4 whole cloves
¼ tsp fennel seeds
¼ tsp black cumin
½ small star anise
1 tbsp (9 g) poppy seeds
1 tbsp (5 g) desiccated coconut
2–3 dried red chilies
¼ tsp peppercorns
1 strand mace
Pinch of nutmeg

SRIRACHA MINT CHUTNEY
1 cup (30 g) tightly packed mint
¼ cup (4 g) cilantro
1 green chili
½ tsp sugar
1 tbsp (15 ml) sriracha (add more if you like it very spicy)
Juice of ½ lemon
¼ cup (60 ml) water
Salt to taste

½ tsp Kashmiri red chili powder
1 tbsp (15 ml) oil
1⅔ cups (400 g) canned brown marrowfat peas, rinsed and drained
3½ cups (350 g) cauliflower florets
2 red onions, cut into quarters
2 carrots, cut into 1–2" (2.5–5-cm) pieces
Salt to taste
10–12 cherry tomatoes
3 nectarines, pitted and quartered

Preheat the oven to 465°F (241°C).

For the spice mix, roast the coriander, green and black cardamom, cinnamon, cloves, fennel, cumin, star anise, poppy seeds, coconut, chilies, peppercorns, mace and nutmeg on medium heat in a pan for a minute or until fragrant. Transfer to a spice grinder and grind to a fine powder.

For the chutney, combine the mint, cilantro, chili, sugar, sriracha, lemon, water and salt in a food processor and process to a thin paste. Mix 3 tablespoons (9 g) of the korma spice mix with the Kashmiri red chili powder into the oil and toss with the marrowfat peas, cauliflower, onions and carrots. Season with salt. Don't add the cherry tomatoes and nectarines yet. Place the vegetables on a baking tray and cover with foil. Bake for 15 minutes. Add the cherry tomatoes and the nectarines to the vegetables and toss a little to mix with the spices. Put back in the oven and bake for an additional 10 minutes.

Serve with the sriracha-spiced mint chutney and hot pooris.

notes: Leftover spices will keep in an airtight container for a few weeks.

If you can't find canned marrowfat peas, use ¾ cup (150 g) dry marrowfat peas, soaked overnight. Rinse the peas and place in a pan with enough water to cover them. Bring to a boil on high heat and simmer, covered, on low heat for 60 to 70 minutes until cooked through. Drain any excess water.

This particular dal has roots in Indonesia and also draws inspiration from a traditional yellow lentil recipe that comes from the state of Gujarat in India. One of the main elements in this dish is the peanut sauce, which was one of the first few things I learned how to make when I came to Holland. This recipe combines both the Indonesian element and Indian spices to make it delightfully textured and delicious and is a perfect example of the versatility of dals.

MASOOR PEANUT SAUCE DAL

Serves 3 to 4

¾ cup (144 g) red lentils (split masoor dal)

2 cups (480 ml) water

Salt to taste

PEANUT SAUCE

1 tsp oil

½ onion, finely chopped

1 clove garlic, crushed

2 tbsp (10 g) desiccated coconut

2 tbsp (30 ml) water

¼ cup (60 ml) coconut milk

2 tbsp (30 ml) peanut butter

2 tsp (10 ml) sambal (or any chili paste)

1½ tsp (7 g) brown sugar

1 tbsp (15 ml) kecap manis (or any sweet soy sauce)

½ tsp lime juice

TEMPERING

2 tbsp (30 ml) oil

1 tsp mustard seeds

1 heaped tbsp (10 g) unsalted peanuts

3–4 cloves garlic, sliced

2 green chilies, slit lengthwise

8–10 curry leaves

½ tsp Kashmiri chili powder

2 heaped tbsp (25 g) raisins

Rinse the lentils a few times under cold water. In a pot, combine the lentils with the water and bring to a boil over high heat. Once the lentils come to a boil, lower the heat to low. Remove any foam with a spoon. Simmer, covered, for around 10 minutes, adding additional water if needed, only enough to barely cover the lentils. Take the lentils off the heat once cooked and set aside. Do not drain.

While the lentils are cooking, make the peanut sauce by heating the oil in a pan. Once the oil is hot, lower the heat to medium and add the onion and the garlic. Cook until they are slightly browned, about a minute. Add the desiccated coconut and fry for another minute. Add the water and cook until the water has evaporated, around 2 minutes. Lower the heat to low and add the coconut milk and cook for another minute. Add the peanut butter, stirring hard to mix it in. Add the sambal, brown sugar, kecap manis and lime juice and mix well while still on low heat. Cook for another minute and then set aside to cool for 2 to 3 minutes.

Add the peanut sauce to the cooked lentils and season with salt. If the lentils are too thick, you can add a little water, depending on how thick or thin you want it. If the lentils are too thin, cook the lentils on low heat while you prepare your tempering.

For the tempering, heat the oil in a wok or pan, and add the mustard seeds, peanuts, garlic, chilies and curry leaves. Once the mustard seeds sputter, after a few seconds, stir vigorously and add the Kashmiri chili powder and the raisins, cooking for less than a minute while still stirring. Immediately add this to the peanut sauce and lentils mixture and stir to mix.

Serve hot with basmati rice.

note: *Tempering, or* tadka *in Hindi, is an essential part of Indian cooking. It is usually added right in the beginning or at the end of a dish depending on what kind of dish it is. Tempering not only adds more oomph to a dish by making it extra flavorful, but it also helps add more nutrients to your dish.*

This recipe is for all green lovers like me *and* my baby girl who is weird like me and loves anything green! Mustard greens (sarson) are commonly used in a popular dish made with a ton of butter and eaten in the cold winter months in Punjab, not only for its flavor but also for its immense health benefits. This dish is made healthier with no butter. The addition of urad dal (whole black gram) replaces the butter with its own buttery, nutty flavor combined with spices used in making pickles. This recipe is a great weeknight dinner not only because it is quick, but also because you need little else with it. Scoop up with papadums or just plain sourdough bread.

URAD SARSON DAL

Serves 3 to 4

1 cup (216 g) whole black gram beans (whole urad dal), soaked overnight

3 cups (720 ml) vegetable broth or water

MUSTARD GREENS

3 cups (170 g) mustard greens

3 cups (90 g) spinach

2 tbsp (30 g) coconut oil

2 tsp (4 g) panch phoron spice

1 clove garlic, cut roughly lengthwise

2 onions, chopped

½"(13-mm) piece ginger, cut into thin strips

1 green chili, slit lengthwise

½ tsp turmeric powder

Salt to taste

TEMPERING

2 tbsp (30 g) coconut oil

1 tsp panch phoron spice

2–3 cloves garlic, cut roughly lengthwise

1 onion, sliced

1 tsp mustard seeds

2 green chilies, slit lengthwise

1 dried red chili

1 tsp Kashmiri chili powder

½ medium tomato, sliced

Rinse the soaked black gram beans under cold water several times. Place in a pan with the vegetable broth or water on high heat until it comes to a boil. Lower the heat and simmer, covered, for 25 to 30 minutes, until the beans are cooked. Add more water as needed, just enough to cover the beans. When cooked they will not be mushy but will have a slight bite to them. Do not drain.

While the beans are cooking, blanch the mustard greens and the spinach. Once done, squeeze out most, but not all, of the excess liquid, blitz to a puree in a food processor and set aside.

Heat the oil in a pan on high heat and add the panch phoron spice mix. Once they start to sputter, lower the heat to medium and add the garlic and the chopped onions. Cook until the garlic and the onions turn slightly brown, around 2 minutes. Add the ginger, chili and turmeric and cook for a few minutes. Add the pureed mustard green mixture and cook for around 10 minutes on low heat. Add salt if needed.

Prepare the tempering by heating the oil in a pan. Once hot, add the panch phoron spice mix. When the spices start to sputter, in about a minute, add the garlic and the onion and cook until the garlic and onion turn slightly brown, 2 to 3 minutes. Add the mustard seeds, green chilies, dried red chili and the chili powder and cook for another 2 to 3 minutes on medium-high heat, stirring continuously. Add the sliced tomato last and cook them very slightly—they should not turn mushy.

Add the cooked beans to the mustard green mixture. Season with salt, stir to mix and cook for another 2 to 3 minutes. Add the hot tempering spices to the greens, mix in and serve hot with papadum or sourdough bread.

note: *If using a pressure cooker, add the beans with the water. Close the lid of the cooker, and give 2 to 3 whistles on high heat. Reduce the heat to low and cook for 10 minutes. Turn off the heat and set aside. Do not drain.*

Whenever I came home from school, if the fragrance of yellow lentils floated to my nose as I walked through the door, my day was made. If I could have, I would have eaten them every day as a child because of how comforting they are. Yellow lentils are cheap, easy to make and can be prepared really quickly too. The mango is used to add a tangy flavor and the black quinoa adds texture and crunch to this dish, making it an interesting relative of the original.

RAW MANGO QUINOA TOOR DAL

Serves 3 to 4

1 cup (205 g) split pigeon peas (toor dal), soaked for 30 minutes

1 cup (165 g) raw mango cubes

3 cups (720 ml) vegetable broth or water

QUINOA
½ cup (85 g) black quinoa

1 cup (240 ml) water

TEMPERING
2 tbsp (30 ml) oil

¾ tsp mustard seeds

1½ tsp (3 g) cumin powder

Pinch of asafetida

5–6 cloves garlic, cut lengthwise

8–10 curry leaves (fresh or dried)

2 dried red chilies

2 medium onions, sliced

2–3 green chilies, slit lengthwise

2 tsp (5 g) red chili powder

Salt to taste
Juice of ½ lime (optional)

Rinse the soaked split pigeon peas in cold water several times. Place them and the cubed mango in a pan with the broth on high heat and bring to a boil. Remove any foam with a spoon. Lower the heat and simmer, covered, for 20 to 25 minutes, adding additional water if needed and only enough to just barely cover the split pigeon peas. Stir occasionally. When done, remove from the heat and do not drain.

Rinse the quinoa several times and add it to a pan with the water. Bring to a boil on high heat. Lower the heat to low and cover the pan. Cook for 15 to 20 minutes or until the quinoa is cooked and the water has evaporated.

For the tempering, heat the oil in a pan on medium heat and add the mustard seeds, cumin, asafetida, garlic, curry leaves, red chilies, onions, green chilies and chili powder. Cook until the onions are nice and brown, 5 to 7 minutes.

Swirl the black quinoa into the split peas, season with salt and add the tempering. Add the lime juice, if using, and stir to combine. Serve hot with white basmati rice.

note: If using a pressure cooker, add the peas and mango with the broth or water. Close the lid of the cooker, and give 2 to 3 whistles on high heat. Reduce the heat to low and cook for 7 to 8 minutes. Turn off the heat and set aside. Do not drain.

Most meals in India are served with chutney as a regular and popular condiment. Of all the chutneys that exist, cilantro chutney is by far the best. It was only natural then to combine it with a legume. I have made this chutney more pesto-like for a creamier and spicier effect as a base for the very attractive butter beans. This dish is ready within 15 minutes and requires so little effort that it will quickly become a weeknight favorite.

CILANTRO CHUTNEY PESTO & SPINACH VAAL DAL

Serves 3 to 4

3⅓ cups (800 g) canned butter beans, rinsed

CILANTRO CHUTNEY PESTO
1 cup (16 g) packed fresh cilantro leaves

¼ cup (30 g) pine nuts

3 green chilies

3 cloves garlic

½"(13-mm) piece ginger

Juice of ½ lemon

⅓ cup (80 ml) olive oil

Salt and pepper to taste

1 tbsp (15 ml) olive oil

1 tsp cumin seeds

2 carrots, sliced in circles

3 cups (90 g) spinach

Rinse the butter beans well under cold water and set aside.

For the pesto, blend the cilantro, pine nuts, chilies, garlic, ginger, lemon, oil, salt and pepper in a food processor until smooth. Set aside.

Heat the olive oil in a pan on medium heat and add the cumin seeds. When they start to sputter, after about 30 seconds, add the carrots and cook for 3 to 4 minutes or until the carrots are slightly charred. Add the butter beans and mix well. Cook for 4 to 5 minutes. Add the spinach leaves and wait for them to wilt, about a minute. Then add the chutney pesto, salt and pepper and stir to mix well.

Take off the heat and sprinkle with sun-dried tomatoes and pine nuts. Decorate with cilantro leaves. Can be served hot or cold with salad.

I have always loved sweet and savory together. I like it in almost everything I eat. We Indians have a little bit of that in our cuisine too, but no one does sweet and savory like the Dutch in my opinion. I thought they were crazy when I was first served a savory dish with some sweet applesauce on the side. But once I had tried it, there was no going back. The buttery navy beans with the bittersweet, spicy Brussels sprouts and the applesauce is a surprise you should not miss.

GARAM MASALA BRUSSELS SPROUTS & NAVY BEAN CURRY *with* APPLESAUCE

Serves 4

APPLESAUCE
1 tsp olive oil

2 apples, peeled, cored and cut into small cubes

Juice of ½ lime

1 tbsp (13 g) sugar

4–5 whole cloves

1 star anise

1 piece cinnamon

1 tbsp (15 ml) water

BRUSSELS SPROUTS MARINADE
1 tsp olive oil

1 tsp garam masala

1½ tsp (3 g) cumin powder

1 tsp Kashmiri chili powder

2 tbsp (30 ml) maple syrup

Salt and pepper to taste

1 lb (454 g) Brussels sprouts, trimmed and halved lengthwise

BRUSSELS SPROUTS & NAVY BEAN FRY
1⅓ cups (350 g) canned navy beans

1 tbsp (15 ml) olive oil

2 shallots, chopped fine

1½ tsp (5 g) nigella seeds (kalonji)

Salt to taste

To make the applesauce, add the oil, apples, lime juice, sugar, cloves, star anise, cinnamon and water to a deep nonstick pan and slowly cook the apples on low heat for 10 to 15 minutes with the lid on. Keep checking from time to time and add more water if it goes too dry, 1 tablespoon (15 ml) at a time. Once the apples are completely soft, mash them up and take off the fire. Set aside to cool.

In a pan big enough to fit the Brussels sprouts, heat the oil on low heat. If you don't have a big enough pan, do it in two batches. While the oil gets hot, combine the garam masala, cumin, chili powder, maple syrup, salt and pepper. Toss the Brussels sprouts with the spice mixture. Place the sprouts cut side down and fry each side for 2 to 3 minutes on medium-high heat, or until slightly charred. Take off the heat and set aside.

Rinse the navy beans well under cold water and set them aside.

In a deep pan, heat the oil on high heat. Once the oil is hot, add the shallots and the nigella seeds. Lower the heat to medium and fry until the shallots are soft and slightly brown, 2 to 3 minutes. Add the navy beans and fry for another few minutes. Last, add the Brussels sprouts to the beans, season with salt if needed and mix to combine well. Garnish with some strips of fresh green apple and micro greens.

Serve hot with basmati rice and applesauce on the side.

This dish is another version of an old favorite dish of *aloo matar* (potatoes and peas). This particular version is made with the addition of tomatoes and is spicy but not hot. You will love how your mind tries to distinguish all the many flavors that your taste buds experience. This rendition is a must if you desire spicy on an otherwise dull weeknight.

SPICY GREEN PEAS, POTATO & BELL PEPPER CURRY

Serves 3 to 4

ROASTED SPICE MIX

2 tbsp (10 g) coriander seeds

½ tsp fennel seeds

½ tsp cumin seeds

1 green cardamom pod

2 whole cloves

5–6 whole pink peppercorns

GREEN PEAS, POTATOES & PEPPER CURRY

1 cup (135 g) frozen green peas

2 medium-size potatoes, peeled and cut into cubes

2 medium tomatoes

6 tbsp (90 g) oil, divided

½ medium red bell pepper, cut into cubes

½ medium yellow bell pepper, cut into cubes

1 medium onion, chopped fine

½" (13-mm) piece ginger, grated

3–4 cloves garlic, minced

3 tbsp (45 ml) tomato paste

½ tsp turmeric powder

¼ tsp Kashmiri chili powder (⅛ tsp if using regular chili powder)

½ cup (120 ml) water

Salt to taste

For the spice mix, roast the coriander, fennel, cumin, cardamom, cloves and peppercorns in a pan on medium heat, stirring often until the spices are fragrant and browning slightly, around a minute. Grind the spices to a coarse powder using a spice grinder or mortar and pestle and set aside.

Cover the green peas with water and leave them to thaw. Bring a pot of water to a boil. Add the potatoes to the boiling water and cook for 2 to 3 minutes so that they are only slightly cooked.

Puree the tomatoes in a food processor and set aside.

Heat 2 tablespoons (30 ml) of oil in a wok on medium-high heat. Once hot, add the cooked potatoes and cook with the lid on for 4 to 5 minutes or until the potatoes are somewhat browned. Stir regularly to prevent the potatoes from burning. Add the red and yellow bell peppers and cook for 2 to 3 minutes. Transfer the potatoes and peppers to a dish and set aside.

In the same pan, heat the rest of the oil. Once hot, add the onion and cook until the onion is soft and starts to brown, 2 to 3 minutes, on medium heat. Add the ginger and garlic and cook until the raw smell of the ginger and garlic disappears and the onions are browning fast, another 2 minutes. Add the tomato puree, tomato paste, turmeric, Kashmiri chili powder and the roasted spice mixture and cook, stirring often, until you see some oil releasing from the sides, about 5 minutes.

Lower the heat, add the bell peppers and the potatoes and stir to mix all elements well. Add the water and simmer, covered, for around 5 minutes or until the pepper and potatoes are cooked through. Drain the water out of the green peas and add them last to the potato and pepper curry. Mix well and cook for an additional few minutes. Season with salt if needed.

Take off the heat, garnish with fresh or thawed frozen green peas, chopped cilantro and some pickled ginger. Serve with hot paranthas.

Most people think that Indian food doesn't believe in simple. This is a myth because my mom was fantastic at making quick, everyday meals. Indian taste buds are used to complex flavors and hot spices. But I think you can have the same effect with minimal spices too. This is one such dish. This recipe is simple, delicious and healthy, can come together very quickly and is a perfect example of how full of flavor vegan food can be. The coconut rice, laced with lentils, is refreshing with the charred vegetables, and the vinaigrette brings it together with its tangy flavors.

CHARRED POPPY SEED CARROTS & CAULIFLOWER FLORETS *with* COCONUT LENTIL RICE & POPPY SEED VINAIGRETTE

Serves 3 to 4

GINGER POPPY SEED VINAIGRETTE
1 shallot, finely chopped
1 tbsp (15 ml) white vinegar
1 tsp Dijon mustard
2 tsp (9 g) sugar
1 tsp poppy seeds
¼ tsp mustard seeds
¼ tsp coriander powder
Pinch of red chili powder
1 tsp ginger, grated
1 tbsp (15 ml) olive oil

1½ lbs (680 g) carrots
1½ cups (150 g) cauliflower florets or broccolini

COCONUT LENTIL RICE
1 tbsp (15 g) coconut oil
1 tsp mustard seeds
2 green chilies, cut lengthwise

1 dried red chili
10–12 curry leaves
1 tbsp (14 g) white lentils (split and dehusked urad dal), soaked in water for 10 minutes
2 tbsp (25 g) split chickpeas (chana dal), soaked in water for 10 minutes
1 cup (85 g) desiccated coconut (use freshly grated if possible)
2 cups (370 g) cooked rice
Salt to taste

3 tbsp (45 ml) olive oil, divided
1 tsp poppy seeds
½ tsp mustard seeds
Salt and pepper to taste

(continued)

CHARRED POPPY SEED CARROTS & CAULIFLOWER FLORETS *with* COCONUT LENTIL RICE & POPPY SEED VINAIGRETTE (cont.)

For the vinaigrette, place the shallot, vinegar, mustard, sugar, poppy seeds, mustard seeds, coriander, chili powder, ginger and oil into a small dish and mix until fully combined. Keep excess in a sealed container in the refrigerator for up to three days.

Peel and trim the carrots but leave them whole. Wash the carrots and the florets/broccolini and set aside to dry.

For the coconut lentil rice, add the oil to a pan and add the mustard seeds, green chilies, dried red chili and the curry leaves. Cook for a minute or so on medium heat. Drain the lentils and split chickpeas and add to this mix. Cook until the chickpeas turn slightly brown, about a minute. Add the coconut and the cooked rice. Stir to mix everything together. Taste and add salt if needed.

In a shallow pan, drizzle 2 tablespoons (30 ml) of olive oil over the carrots and the florets/broccolini. Rub with your fingers so the vegetables are well coated.

In another pan, heat the remaining oil with the poppy seeds and mustard seeds, and add any additional oil left over after rubbing on the vegetables, on high heat. Add the carrots and the florets and continue to cook on high heat. After around 5 minutes, reduce the heat to medium and continue to cook the vegetables until charred on all sides. This should take another 5 to 6 minutes. Once done, add salt and pepper and toss to mix. Turn off the heat and transfer the carrots to a chopping board and cut each carrot into roughly three angled pieces.

Serve the carrots and the cauliflower florets hot on a bed of coconut lentil rice, drizzle the poppy seed vinaigrette and garnish with toasted coconut and peanuts.

Fasting in India is not just a religious thing. It has logic in its historical traditions and health benefits. I remember Mom fasting on Tuesdays and I remember her telling me that a day without all the food made her feel rejuvenated and happy the next day. To break her fast she used to make a tomato dish, which was sweet and tangy and just out of this world. Even though my mom doesn't fast anymore and doesn't remember how she made the tomato curry, just talking about this beautiful dish with her brought back sweet memories. This is my version of what I remember. Growing up, Mom also gave me two or three dried figs every day, first thing in the morning because they are powerhouses of nutrients. I added them to this curry to give it body and crunch.

TANGY TOMATO & FIG CURRY

Serves 4

ROASTED CHERRY TOMATOES
1⅔ cups (250 g) cherry tomatoes
1 tbsp (15 ml) olive oil
Salt and pepper

ROASTED SPICES
¼ tsp mustard seeds
¼ tsp nigella seeds (kalonji)
1 tsp fennel seeds
½ tsp poppy seeds

TOMATO CURRY
4 tbsp (60 ml) oil
2 small onions, sliced
3–4 cloves garlic, crushed
½" (13-mm) piece ginger, crushed
1 tsp turmeric powder
1 tsp chili powder

2 green chilies, chopped
2 tsp (8 g) coconut sugar
⅓ cup (50 g) dried figs, sliced
4 cups (720 g) quartered tomatoes
Salt to taste

TEMPERING
1 tbsp (15 ml) oil
Pinch of asafetida
1 tsp mustard seeds
½ tsp fenugreek seeds
6–8 curry leaves

Bread/cooked basmati rice

(continued)

TANGY TOMATO & FIG CURRY (cont.)

Preheat the oven to 400°F (205°C). Line a baking sheet with parchment paper. Place the cherry tomatoes on the sheet and drizzle with the oil. Rub it on the surface of the tomatoes a little bit. Sprinkle with salt and pepper and bake for 10 minutes. Take out of the oven and set aside.

While the tomatoes are in the oven, dry roast the mustard, nigella, fennel and poppy seeds for a minute in a pan on medium-high heat until fragrant. Make sure to stir often so that the spices don't get burnt. Take off the heat and grind to a fine powder using a spice grinder or mortal and pestle.

For the curry, heat the oil in a pan on high heat. Once hot, add the onions. Cook until the onions start to brown, 2 to 3 minutes. Lower the heat to medium and add the garlic and ginger and cook until the raw smell of the garlic and ginger is gone, 2 to 3 minutes. Add the roasted spices along with the turmeric, chili powder, chilies and sugar, stir to mix well and let the spices cook for a few minutes. Add the figs and quartered tomatoes and cook on low heat for 18 to 20 minutes or until most tomatoes are mush but have not lost their shape completely. Add salt and turn off the heat once ready. Add the roasted cherry tomatoes to the curry.

For the tempering, heat the oil in a pan and add the asafetida, mustard, fenugreek seeds and curry leaves. Cook on medium heat. Once the mustard seeds sputter, in about a minute, turn off the heat and add immediately to the tomato curry. You don't need to mix it in because it will seep in.

Garnish with figs and scoop with or top on fresh bread. Alternatively, this can also be eaten with plain rice.

Brown lentils (whole masoor dal) is a favorite in my house. There are no real lentils that can top this one. Not for my daughter anyway! So, I can never go wrong when this dal is on the menu at any meal. I use a lot of tomatoes in this version and the tempering has a ton of shallots. I added blanched sugar snap peas as a garnish for a surprising crunch that will wow you. This is a hearty lentil dish, one that can be eaten just by itself by scooping it up with a slice of bread.

MASOOR DAL *with* SPICY SHALLOTS TEMPERING & SUGAR SNAP PEAS

Serves 2 to 3

BROWN LENTILS
½ cup (96 g) brown lentils (whole masoor dal), soaked for 8–10 hours

3 cups (720 ml) water

2 tbsp (30 ml) olive oil

1 medium red onion, chopped

1"(2.5-cm) piece ginger, cut into strips

1 tomato, chopped

3 tbsp (45 ml) tomato paste

1 tsp Italian spices

Salt and pepper to taste

SHALLOT TEMPERING
3 tbsp (45 ml) olive oil

1 tsp cumin seeds

4–5 curry leaves

3–4 cloves garlic, cut in half lengthwise

2 green chilies, slit lengthwise

1 dried red chili

10–12 small round shallots, peeled but kept whole

Pinch of asafetida

1 tsp brown sugar

2 tbsp (30 ml) olive oil, divided

Sugar snap peas

Rinse the lentils under cold water. In a pot, combine them with the water and bring to a boil over high heat. Once they come to a boil, lower the heat to low. Remove any foam with a spoon. Simmer, covered, for around 30 minutes. Take the lentils off the heat once cooked. Do not drain.

While the lentils are cooking, heat the oil in a pan on high heat. Once hot, add the onion and the ginger. Cook until the onions get soft and slightly brown and the raw smell of ginger is gone, 2 to 3 minutes. Lower the heat to medium and add the tomato, tomato paste and the Italian spices. Cook while stirring for another 4 to 5 minutes or until the tomatoes are somewhat mushy and a little bit charred. Add the cooked lentils and the salt and pepper to taste and cook until the lentils are well combined with the tomato mixture, 5 to 6 minutes. Lower the heat to low and let the lentils simmer while you make the tempering.

For the tempering, heat the oil in a pan on high heat. Once hot, add the cumin seeds. When they start to sputter, after a few seconds, add the curry leaves, garlic and green and red chilies. Lower the heat to medium and continue to stir and cook until the raw smell of the garlic is gone and it has turned slightly brown, 1 to 2 minutes. Add the shallots with the asafetida and the sugar and turn up the heat to medium-high. Stir often and cook until the shallots are nicely caramelized, around 5 minutes.

Add this shallot tempering to the simmering lentils and mix well. Season with salt and pepper and let the lentils continue to simmer.

Heat 1 tablespoon (15 ml) of oil in a pan and sauté the sugar snap peas for a quick minute or two on high heat. Take off the heat and cut each pea pod into 2 to 3 pieces at an angle.

Take the lentils off the heat and drizzle with the remaining olive oil. Dress the dish with the sugar snap peas, cherry tomatoes and cilantro.

Growing up, I only liked pineapples in small quantities. I certainly couldn't just sit and eat slices of it. Its flavor is much too strong for me, but in curries it lends the most amazing flavor. This curry is originally made with mangoes. I had never heard of it until recently when I visited Kerala and discovered how they combined a fruit with coconut in the most beautiful marriage between sweet, creamy and spicy. Pineapple works wonderfully as a replacement for the mango, and I realized I could eat piece after piece of it cooked this way.

SWEET CHILI COCONUT PINEAPPLE CURRY

Serves 3 to 4

PINEAPPLE CURRY

½ ripe pineapple, cut into square chunks

5–6 tbsp (70–85 g) jaggery

2 tsp (5 g) Kashmiri chili powder

½ tsp turmeric powder

Salt to taste

¼ cup (60 ml) water

SPICE MIX

1 cup (80 g) fresh grated coconut

1 medium onion

1 green chili

½" (13-mm) piece ginger

1 clove garlic

¼ tsp cumin powder

½ tsp Kashmiri chili powder

¼ tsp turmeric powder

½ cup (120 ml) coconut milk

TEMPERING

1 tbsp (15 ml) oil

1–2 shallots, sliced fine

½ tsp mustard seeds

¼ tsp fenugreek seeds

2–3 dried red chilies

1 sprig curry leaves

In a pan, add the pineapple with the jaggery, Kashmiri chili powder, turmeric and salt. Add the water and cook for around 15 minutes or until the spices are infused into the pineapple, on low heat.

For the spice mix, grind the coconut, onion, chili, ginger, garlic, cumin, chili powder and turmeric using a spice grinder or mortar and pestle. Add a little water to make a fine paste.

Stir the ground spice paste into the pineapple mix and cook for another 5 to 6 minutes.

Add the coconut milk and mix well again. Cook for about 5 minutes. (The cooking time for this curry may vary by 5 to 10 minutes, depending on how ripe your pineapple is. If your pineapple is very ripe, then reduce cooking time and if less ripe, increase the cooking time.)

For the tempering, heat the oil in a pan on medium heat and add the shallots, mustard and fenugreek seeds and the red chilies. Fry until the shallots turn a beautiful golden brown, 3 to 4 minutes. Add the curry leaves and fry for a few seconds, stirring continuously. Mix immediately with the pineapple coconut curry and season with salt.

Serve hot with plain basmati rice.

note: Jaggery is an unrefined sugar that is very popular in India and South Asia. In India we sometimes just eat it by itself. It has a warm earthy caramel taste that is quite addictive. Because it is unrefined it retains some nutrients that white sugar doesn't. It usually just comes in a big chunk that you can grate like I do, although the powdered variety is also available and is just as good and saves valuable time.

I have been making this dish for years, and it is my daughter's favorite Indian dish. She has been calling it yellow balls since I can remember. These chickpeas are unlike how we prepare it in North India where it is almost always prepared with gravy and slowly cooked for hours. This particular version using canned chickpeas can be ready within 15 minutes. It is my perfect go-to meal when I am tired and want a quick meal that is healthy and heavenly in taste.

GINGER TURMERIC CHICKPEAS
with ROASTED CHERRY TOMATOES

Serves 3 to 4

ROASTED CHERRY TOMATOES
1⅓ cups (200 g) cherry tomatoes

1 tbsp (15 ml) olive oil

Salt and pepper

CHICKPEAS
3 cups (720 g) canned chickpeas

2 tbsp (30 ml) olive oil

1 medium red onion, sliced

1" (2.5-cm) piece ginger, cut into strips

1 tsp turmeric powder

1 tsp cumin powder

Salt to taste

Preheat the oven to 400°F (205°C).

Prepare a baking sheet lined with parchment paper. Place the cherry tomatoes on the baking sheet and drizzle with olive oil. Sprinkle with salt and pepper and bake for 10 minutes.

While the tomatoes are roasting, rinse the chickpeas under cold water. Heat the oil in a pan on high heat. Once hot, add the onion and the ginger and cook until the onion begins to brown at the edges, 2 to 3 minutes. Lower the heat to medium and add the chickpeas to the onions and ginger and stir to mix. Cook for 2 to 3 minutes. Add the turmeric and cumin. Stir the spices into the chickpeas, cover and cook for 10 to 12 minutes on low heat. Add the salt and roasted cherry tomatoes and cook for another minute or two.

Garnish with red onion and cilantro sprinkled on top.

Even though we use fennel seeds a lot in Indian food, we don't use fennel bulb at all to my knowledge. Maybe because the part of India I grew up in is warm and fennel is mostly a winter vegetable. I discovered this vegetable in Holland and was fascinated by the licorice flavor it brought forth when cooked. It lends itself very well to curry, especially when combined with all sorts of fragrant Indian spices. The sweet flavor of the fennel is beautifully offset with the blistered chili peppers, bringing spice to the sweet in a lovely balance of flavors. This is a meaty vegan dish and will satisfy those who are new to the vegan diet.

BRAISED FENNEL CURRY IN PICKLING SPICES *with* BLISTERED CHILI PEPPERS

Serves 4

ROASTED SPICE MIX
¼ tsp fenugreek seeds
¼ tsp nigella seeds (kalonji)
1 tsp fennel seeds
1 tsp coriander seeds
1 tsp cumin seeds
½ tsp turmeric powder
Juice of ½ lime

BRAISED FENNEL CURRY
1 medium fennel bulb (or 2 small ones)
4 tbsp (60 ml) oil, divided
1 tsp cumin seeds
2–3 cloves garlic, cut into 3 parts
1" (2.5-cm) piece ginger, cut into strips

1 large onion, cut into thick slices
Salt to taste
3 carrots, cut into 2" (5-cm) angled pieces
½ cup (120 ml) tomato puree
1 tbsp (15 ml) tomato paste
2 tbsp (26 g) coconut sugar
2 tbsp (30 ml) coconut milk
¼ cup (60 ml) water

BLISTERED CHILI PEPPERS
1 tbsp (15 ml) oil
4 large green chili peppers

(continued)

For the spice mix, in a pan over medium-high heat, dry roast the fenugreek, nigella, fennel, coriander and cumin seeds until fragrant, about 1 minute. Take off the heat and grind to a fine powder using a spice grinder or mortar and pestle. Add the turmeric powder and the lime juice. Mix and set aside.

Remove the tops of the fennel bulb, reserving the fennel fronds for decoration. Slice off a bit of the bottom that is the hard root. Then cut the bulb in half and quarter the halves. Remove any wilted bruised parts. Heat 1 tablespoon (15 ml) of oil in a wide shallow pan on high heat. Once hot, place the fennel wedges in the pan, cover with a lid and cook for 3 to 4 minutes per side on medium-high heat, or until the fennel looks nice and brown. Watch carefully and turn so that all the sides get browned. Transfer to a dish and set aside.

In the same pan, heat the rest of the oil on high heat and add the cumin seeds. Once they start to sputter, after a few seconds, add the garlic and the ginger and reduce the heat to medium. Cook the ginger and garlic until the raw smell disappears and the garlic looks slightly brown, 2 to 3 minutes. Add the sliced onion and season with salt, then cook for 3 to 4 minutes or until the onion is soft and starts to brown. Add the roasted spice mixture and stir to combine. Lower the heat to low and cook this spice mix for a few minutes.

Add the carrots and stir to coat them with all the spices. Cook for around 5 minutes and then add the tomato puree, tomato paste, coconut sugar, coconut milk and the water. Mix well and add the fennel wedges. Cover the pan with a lid and let simmer for 12 to 15 minutes or until the fennel and the carrots are soft but not mushy.

While the curry is simmering, make the blistered chili peppers by heating the oil in a pan on high heat. Add the whole chili peppers and cook while occasionally flipping the peppers. Once the peppers are discolored and the skin starts to peel a little bit, in 2 to 3 minutes, turn off the heat and add the peppers to the curry.

Serve garnished with the fennel fronds and mint leaves.

Visually rhubarb is one of the most beautiful fruits I have seen. I am partial to fruits and vegetables that color everything along with them. Rhubarb in a curry may sound strange, but you have to try it to believe how good it tastes. The tartness combines wonderfully with the raspberries, making this dish excitingly sweet and tangy. The cauliflower carries the curry flavors into this colorful plate of food, which is deliciously offset by the fruitiness of the rest of the flavors.

RHUBARB & RASPBERRY CURRY with ROASTED CAULIFLOWER

Serves 3 to 4

ROASTED CURRY POWDER
1 tbsp (5 g) coriander seeds
1 tbsp (6 g) cumin seeds
1 tsp whole black peppercorns
1 tsp mustard seeds
1 tsp fenugreek seeds
2–3 dried red chilies
½ tsp turmeric powder

ROASTED CAULIFLOWER
1 tbsp (15 ml) oil
Juice of ½ orange
Salt and pepper
3½ cups (350 g) cauliflower florets

CURRY
2 tbsp (30 ml) oil
1 tbsp (9 g) black sesame seeds
1 medium onion, sliced
1" (2.5-cm) piece ginger, sliced in strips
4–5 stalks rhubarb, cut roughly into ½" (13-mm) pieces
1 cup (123 g) raspberries, frozen or fresh
½ cup (120 ml) water
1 tbsp (15 ml) red wine vinegar
1 clove garlic, crushed
3–4 tbsp (42–56 g) brown sugar (more or less based on rhubarb sourness)

(continued)

RHUBARB & RASPBERRY CURRY *with* ROASTED CAULIFLOWER (cont.)

Preheat the oven to 405°F (207°C).

To make the curry powder, in a pan on medium heat, dry roast the coriander, cumin, peppercorns, mustard, fenugreek seeds and chilies around 1 minute until fragrant, making sure you stir continuously. Once done, add the turmeric and mix well. Set aside. Any leftover curry powder will keep well for a few weeks in an airtight container.

For the roasted cauliflower, in a mixing bowl combine the oil with orange juice, 1 tablespoon (3 g) of the curry powder and the salt and pepper. Mix well. Toss the cauliflower florets in the mixture and lay out on a baking sheet. Bake for 20 to 25 minutes or until the cauliflower is cooked through and slightly charred.

While the cauliflower bakes, make the curry by heating the oil in a pan on medium-high heat. Once hot, add the sesame seeds and stir. After around a minute, add the onion and ginger. Cook until the onion becomes transparent and starts to brown, 4 to 5 minutes. Add the rhubarb pieces, raspberries and water and let it simmer on low heat for 6 to 8 minutes. Add the vinegar, garlic and sugar. Mix well again and cook for another few minutes until the rhubarb has fallen apart and has combined with the raspberries.

Once the cauliflower is done, add it to the rhubarb curry. Serve hot with rice.

Every time Mom decided to make *patta gobi* (potatoes and cabbage) in the winter, my sister and I knew it was because she didn't feel like cooking that day or because she was so sick and tired of that dreaded, "What should we make for dinner today?" question. There was a substantial lack of variety in the vegetables where we lived during those cold months. Cabbage was her I-don't-feel-like-cooking-today vegetable because of how fast it could be prepared, requiring very little effort. This is my version of that simple dish that I changed using parsnips—a vegetable that we don't get in India as far as I know.

CHINESE CABBAGE CURRY *with* PARSNIPS & RAISINS

Serves 4

2 tbsp (30 g) coconut oil

1½ tsp (5 g) mustard seeds

8–10 curry leaves

3–4 parsnips, peeled and cut into rounds

1 Chinese cabbage, sliced fine

2 tsp (10 g) jaggery

Salt to taste

4 tbsp (20 g) desiccated coconut

¼ cup (40 g) raisins

In a pan, heat the oil on high heat. Once hot, add the mustard seeds. Once they start to sputter, after a few seconds, lower the heat to medium and add the curry leaves. Once the curry leaves change their color slightly, after a few seconds, add the parsnips. Cook the parsnips on high heat, stirring continuously until they begin to brown at the edges, 4 to 5 minutes. Add the cabbage and stir continuously again for 3 to 4 minutes.

Lower the heat to medium and add the jaggery and the salt. Continue to cook for another 4 to 5 minutes. Season with more salt. Add the desiccated coconut and raisins and cook for 4 to 5 minutes, stirring occasionally.

Serve garnished with walnuts and pomegranate arils.

Green beans are big in India, especially for vegetarians. They are cheap, very healthy, easy to cook and go with almost any dish. I've added the bell pepper and chili sauce to add some oomph to this nutritious dish. This recipe is a wonderful addition to my weekly dinners because of the speed with which it gets made and how much nourishment it provides.

GREEN BEAN CURRY

Serves 4

3 tbsp (45 ml) oil

2 medium onions, sliced

1"(2.5-cm) piece ginger, cut into strips

3 cloves garlic, crushed

1 tsp chili powder

½ tsp coriander powder

½ tsp turmeric powder

½ lb (225 g) green beans, stems removed and cut in half

1 yellow bell pepper, cored and cut into strips

1 cup (255 g) canned red kidney beans, rinsed and drained

Salt to taste

1 tsp sambal (or any chili paste)

Heat the oil in a wok on high heat. Once hot, add the sliced onions and cook until the onions begin to brown, 2 to 3 minutes. Lower the heat to medium, and then add the ginger and the crushed garlic and cook until the raw smell of the ginger and garlic is gone, 2 to 3 minutes. Add the chili powder, coriander and turmeric and stir to combine well. Add the green beans, bell pepper strips and the kidney beans. Stir to combine all the spices with the vegetables and beans. Add salt, reduce the heat to low, cover the wok with a lid and cook for 15 to 18 minutes or until the beans are cooked through but not completely soft.

Add the sambal and stir again to combine everything together, cooking for just a minute or two.

Serve hot with plain basmati rice.

Farmers' markets and grocery stores are a big source of inspiration for my dishes, and there is such a huge variety of foods that still need trying. The Romanesco is just such an example. I had never used this vegetable before the testing of this book, but I am hooked. My eyes can't get enough of this beautiful vegetable. I decided to marry it with the chana dal, which is as mundane as it can get. A dash of lemongrass, mixed with my favorite Indian spices, and it was a match made in heaven.

LEMONGRASS TURNIP CHANA DAL *with* ROASTED ROMANESCO

Serves 3 to 4

1 cup (200 g) split chickpeas (chana dal), soaked overnight

2 cups (480 ml) water

LEMONGRASS SPICE MIX

2 green chili peppers

1 shallot

3 cloves garlic

1" (2.5-cm) piece ginger

1 stalk lemongrass

Zest of 1 lime

½ tsp turmeric powder

1 tsp coriander powder

1 head Romanesco, cut into large bite-size florets

5 tbsp (75 ml) olive oil, divided

2 small onions, chopped

1 turnip, cut into small blocks

Salt to taste

TEMPERING

1 tbsp (15 ml) oil

½ tsp red chili powder

Wash and rinse the split chickpeas several times under cold water. In a pan, combine them with the water and bring to a boil on high heat. Lower the heat, simmer, covered, for 20 to 25 minutes or until the lentils are cooked through and soft. Once done, set aside. Do not drain.

For the spice mix, using a food processor or in a mortar and pestle, combine and blitz or crush the chili peppers, shallot, garlic, ginger, lemongrass, lime zest, turmeric and coriander powder. Use a teaspoon of water to make it a smooth paste. Set aside.

While the split chickpeas are cooking, wash the Romanesco florets and pat dry. Heat 3 tablespoons (45 ml) of oil on high heat, in a wide pan with a lid. Once hot, add the Romanesco pieces. Continue to cook the Romanesco on high heat until it starts to get soft and charred, 10 to 12 minutes, tossing every now and then so all sides get browned. Transfer to a dish lined with kitchen towels and set aside.

In the meantime, heat the rest of the olive oil in another pan on high heat. Once hot, add the onions and cook until the onions are transparent and start to brown, around 2 to 3 minutes. Lower the heat to medium and add the lemongrass spice mix and cook for another 2 to 3 minutes, until the spices are fragrant. Add the turnip blocks, cover the pan and cook for around 10 minutes on low heat or until the turnip is cooked through. Last, add the cooked split chickpeas with their liquid and salt. Stir to mix well. Turn off the heat and add the roasted Romanesco pieces and mix.

For the tempering, heat the oil in a pan, add the red chili powder and remove from the heat within 30 seconds. Pour into the turnip chana dal.

Garnish with red onion slices and cilantro and serve with fresh naan.

The first Indian food I served to guests in Holland was a potato dish with asafetida in it. The dish was a success. The Dutch love their potatoes, and they just loved this particular version of simple spiced potatoes. When asked what made them so spectacularly delicious, I told them that one of the ingredients was asafetida. Perplexed expressions followed, as they had no idea what it was. On close inspection I found out that asafetida is *duivelsdrek* in Dutch, which literally means "poop from the devil" or "devil's dung"! It is a strong spice, to be used sparingly, but it lends huge amounts of flavor as it does in this particular case. Add the brown lentils and some bok choy and you have a very satisfying meal on your hands.

ASAFETIDA POTATOES & CARROT CURRY
with BROWN LENTILS & BOK CHOY

Serves 3 to 4

2 tbsp (30 ml) oil

¼ tsp asafetida

1 tsp cumin seeds

½ tsp mustard seeds

1 tsp coriander powder

4–6 curry leaves

1 lb (454 g) potatoes, cut into small chunks

1 cup (125 g) sliced carrots

¾ cup (180 g) canned brown lentils (whole masoor dal), rinsed

½ lb (225 g) bok choy, roughly cut into strips

Salt and pepper to taste

Heat the oil in a wok on high heat. Once hot, add the asafetida and let it cook for 30 seconds. Add the cumin and mustard seeds. When they start to sputter, after a few seconds, add the coriander and the curry leaves. Stir very briefly before adding the potato chunks. Stir to mix the spices with the potatoes, cover the wok and let cook on medium-high heat for 5 to 8 minutes or until the potatoes just begin to brown, stirring often. Add the carrots, mix and cover.

Let cook for around 10 minutes or until the carrots and potatoes are cooked through. Once cooked, add the lentils and the bok choy. Cook until the bok choy has completely wilted, 3 to 4 minutes. Add salt and pepper and serve hot with rotis.

Tamarind has a sweet place in my heart. It brings memories of running around with my bare feet on the cold floor of our house with a piece of tamarind in my mouth, sucking on its sourness with much delight, one eye closed, squealing at how sharp its flavors were. Tamarind is used quite often in Indian cooking exactly for these properties, to give an acidic flavor to the dish. This recipe is delightfully tangy with some sugar thrown in to balance the tartness of this gorgeous fruit. It also forms a lovely union with the potatoes. This dish is a fine representation of not just how scrumptious vegan food is but also shows how many different ways you can cook potatoes.

TAMARIND POTATO CURRY *with* SESAME SEEDS

Serves 3 to 4

1 lb (454 g) small potatoes, peeled
Water to cook

TAMARIND CURRY PASTE
1 tbsp (15 ml) tamarind paste
3 tbsp (45 ml) tomato paste
1 tbsp (15 ml) tomato ketchup
3 cloves garlic, minced
1" (2.5-cm) piece ginger, grated
1 tbsp (9 g) sesame seeds
1 tsp cumin powder
½ tsp red chili powder
1 tsp chili flakes
1 tsp coconut sugar
5–6 tbsp (75–90 ml) water
Salt to taste

2 tbsp (30 ml) oil
Pinch of asafetida
½ tsp nigella seeds (kalonji)
¼ tsp fenugreek seeds
8–10 curry leaves
10–12 cherry tomatoes

In a pan, place the potatoes in enough water to just cover them. Simmer the potatoes on medium-low heat until they are cooked through but don't fall apart, 10 to 15 minutes. If you insert a knife through the potatoes and it goes through with ease, the potatoes are cooked. Drain the water and let the potatoes cool. Once cool, cut in half.

For the tamarind curry paste, in a large bowl, mix together the tamarind paste, tomato paste, ketchup, garlic, ginger, sesame seeds, cumin, chili powder, chili flakes, sugar, water and salt. Stir to combine. Set aside.

Heat the oil in a pan on high heat. Once hot, lower the heat to medium and add the asafetida, nigella and fenugreek seeds. Add the curry leaves after around 30 seconds. Add the tamarind curry mix as soon as the curry leaves begin to sputter. Cook while stirring for a minute or two and then add the potatoes. Stir to mix well and cook on low heat with the lid on. Cook for 10 to 12 minutes or until the potatoes are cooked through. Halfway through, add the cherry tomatoes.

Garnish with some extra sesame seeds and serve hot with a lentil dish and plain white rice.

If I had to pick one dish that was not from North India, where I come from, that makes my mouth salivate like nothing else, I'd pick *sambhar*. Sambhar is a South Indian lentil dish that combines all sorts of vegetables in it. Okra is one of my favorite additions in this dish. In this recipe I have deconstructed the sambhar by making it a dry lentil version with okra forming the central element in the dish. It is scrumptious and has a distinct sambhar flavor.

SAMBHAR SPICED OKRA

Serves 3 to 4

½ cup (96 g) yellow lentils (moong dal), soaked overnight

½ cup (100 g) split chickpeas (chana dal), soaked overnight

4–5 tbsp (60–75 ml) oil

2 tsp (4 g) cumin seeds

¾ tsp mustard seeds

5–6 curry leaves (fresh or dried)

1–2 dried red chilies

2 lbs (907 g) okra, cut in angled pieces

1 tbsp (5 g) coriander powder

Salt and pepper to taste

Wash and rinse the soaked lentils and split chickpeas under cold water a few times. Drain and set aside.

Heat the oil in a pan on high heat. Once hot, add the cumin and mustard seeds. Once they sputter, add the curry leaves. When the curry leaves just begin to sputter and change color, in a few seconds, lower the heat to medium, add the red chilies and a few seconds later add the okra. Add the coriander powder, stir and mix well. Continue to cook on medium heat for 10 to 12 minutes or until the okra is soft and slightly brown at the edges. Add the lentils and chickpeas and continue to cook for 4 to 5 minutes. Season with salt and pepper.

Garnish with cashews, cilantro and sliced red onion. Serve hot with freshly made rotis.

note: *Because okra releases a slimy material, it is important that your okra is completely dry before cooking. Also add salt at the very end of the cooking process.*

My mother tried everything under the sun to get me to eat apples. I wouldn't. I have always been a fussy eater and like my fruits better in curries because of my deep love for the sweet and savory combination. In this case the green apple is delightfully sharp in flavor, and the acidic flavor works very well with the creamy and spicy elements, with all those delicious crunchy veggies on top.

GREEN APPLE CURRY *with* STIR-FRY VEGETABLES

Serves 3 to 4

GREEN APPLESAUCE

1 green apple, peeled and cored or any other tangy apple variety

1 cup (240 ml) coconut yogurt or any other vegan yogurt

3–4 cloves garlic

1"(2.5-cm) piece ginger

1 loosely packed cup (16 g) cilantro leaves

¼ loosely packed cup (6 g) mint leaves

2 green chilies

2–3 spring onions

1 tsp sugar

Salt and pepper to taste

1 tbsp (15 ml) oil

STIR-FRY

3⅓ cups (200 g) sugar snap peas

½ head Romanesco or cauliflower, cut into bite–size florets

1½ cups (150 g) broccolini

1 tbsp (15 ml) olive oil

1 tsp cumin seeds

1 tsp fennel seeds

For the applesauce, put the apple, yogurt, garlic, ginger, cilantro, mint, chilies, onions, sugar, salt and pepper in a food processor and blitz until all the ingredients are combined and pureed to a smooth sauce. Heat the oil in a pan. Once hot, add the sauce and cook for 3 to 4 minutes. Transfer to a bowl and set aside.

Blanch the peas, Romanesco florets and broccolini for 3 to 4 minutes and then run under cold water to stop the cooking process. Set aside.

Heat the oil in a pan on high heat. When hot, add the cumin and fennel seeds. When the cumin seeds start to sputter, after a few seconds, add the vegetables and stir-fry for 4 to 6 minutes. The vegetables should still have a little bite to them.

Divide the green applesauce among the plates and scoop the vegetables on top. Serve hot.

Dals the way we eat them in India would really be considered soups in the West. This dal soup is ready in a jiffy and is made with my all-time favorite dal. Split pigeon peas are great for quick meals because they don't need soaking or any other pre-prep. Soup made with this dal is creamy and tangy and is a fast yummy meal.

TOOR DAL CARROT TURMERIC SOUP

Serves 4

3 tbsp (45 ml) olive oil

1 onion, chopped

1" (2.5-cm) piece ginger, grated

2 cloves garlic, minced

3 carrots, diced

½ tsp turmeric powder

½ tsp coriander powder

1 tsp cumin powder

4 cups (960 ml) broth

1½ cups (307 g) split pigeon peas (toor dal)

Salt and pepper to taste

Juice of ½ lemon

Heat the oil in a deep pan over high heat. Once hot, add the onion, ginger and garlic. Cook until the onion is transparent and the raw smell of the ginger and garlic is gone, 2 to 3 minutes. Lower the heat to medium and add the carrots, turmeric, coriander and cumin and stir well to mix. Cook for a few minutes and then add the broth and the peas. Bring to a boil on high heat and then cover with a lid and let simmer on low heat for 20 to 25 minutes or until the peas are completely cooked.

Use an immersion blender to puree everything until completely smooth. Season with salt and pepper and mix in the lemon juice.

Divide the soup into bowls and garnish with roasted pumpkin seeds, cumin seeds and cilantro.

Kale, or *boerenkool* in Dutch, was deemed the revival vegetable some years ago here in Holland. Just as kale was becoming hip everywhere else in the world, so was it here. Kale has typically been eaten in Holland for hundreds of years and used to be a common winter vegetable. But in recent times it has become extremely fashionable to eat it again.

As an Indian, I had never eaten it before. Kale is my new favorite green. I love how mildly bitter it is and how crunchy, and once I'd tried it, it quickly became a favorite. It works perfectly in this dal alongside the spinach as a leafy green that promises to heal as so many vegetables do.

KALE SPINACH MOONG DAL

Serves 4

1½ cups (310 g) split and dehusked mung beans (split and dehusked moong dal)

4 cups (960 ml) water

1 tsp turmeric powder

1 bay leaf

3 tbsp (45 ml) olive oil

1 tsp mustard seeds

1 tsp cumin seeds

2–3 green chilies, halved

6–8 cloves garlic, crushed

1" (2.5-cm) piece ginger, crushed

¼ tsp turmeric powder

Pinch of asafetida

Salt to taste

1 medium onion, chopped

1 tomato, chopped

4 cups (270 g) kale

½ tsp Kashmiri chili powder

3 cups (90 g) spinach

1 cup (240 ml) water

1 tbsp (2 g) dried fenugreek leaves (kasturi methi)

1 tsp garam masala

Thoroughly rinse the beans in cold water. Combine them with the water, turmeric and bay leaf in a pan and bring to a boil. Remove any foam with a spoon. Reduce the heat and let simmer for 20 minutes or until the water is nearly evaporated and the beans are soft. Turn off the heat and set aside. Do not drain.

While the beans are cooking, in a deep pan, heat the oil on high heat. Once hot, add the mustard seeds. Once they sputter, after a few seconds, add the cumin and green chilies. Add the garlic and ginger after the cumin begins to sputter, in a few seconds. Lower the heat to medium and add the turmeric, asafetida and salt and cook for 1 to 2 minutes while stirring. Add the onion and cook for 2 to 3 minutes or until the onion is transparent, stirring often. Add the tomato and cook until the oil starts to separate on the sides, 4 to 5 minutes.

Next, add the kale and Kashmiri chili powder and stir to mix well. Cook for 2 to 3 minutes before adding the spinach. Add the water and let the kale and spinach simmer on low heat for 5 to 6 minutes or until the greens have completely wilted.

Add the cooked beans to this mixture and bring to a boil and let simmer for 2 to 3 minutes. Turn off the heat and add the fenugreek leaves and the garam masala. Garnish with chopped cilantro and dried lentils and serve hot with plain rice.

note: *Kasturi methi are dried fenugreek leaves that are widely used in Indian cooking to add a creamy flavor to a dish. For me it is a perfect vegan ingredient that replaces any kind of cream used in dishes. It offers a smoky, creamy flavor that you will love.*

I'm going to be honest. I had never tried plantain before the testing for this book. I love fruit in my curries, but bananas? That didn't sound right to me. But I love regular bananas so much, I thought it was worth a try. Plantains are used quite a lot by the Surinamese community in Holland. I don't ever remember seeing plantains being eaten in North India, except in the form of chips, so I didn't grow up eating them. In this version the plantains are wrapped in coconut flour and then deep-fried. This dish is scrumptious, spicy and highly addictive—another meaty and soul-satisfying vegan dish.

SPICY COCONUT PLANTAIN SOY BEAN CURRY

Serves 4

DEEP-FRIED PLANTAINS

1¼ tbsp (9 g) coconut flour

3–4 cloves garlic, minced

1" (2.5-cm) piece ginger, grated

½ tsp chili powder

Salt and pepper to taste

¼ cup (60 ml) water

2 plantains, peeled and cut into 1" (2.5-cm) angled pieces

Oil for deep-frying

CURRY

2 tbsp (30 ml) oil

4–5 dried red chilies

1 tsp mustard seeds

½ tsp cumin seeds

5–6 curry leaves

2–3 green chilies, sliced in half lengthwise

½ tsp white lentils (split and dehusked urad dal)

½ tbsp (6 g) split chickpeas (chana dal)

½ cup (127 g) fresh, shelled soybeans (edamame)

½ tsp turmeric powder

½ tsp chili powder

2 tbsp (2 g) chopped cilantro

2 tbsp (30 ml) coconut milk

Salt and pepper to taste

In a bowl mix the coconut flour, garlic, ginger, chili powder and the salt and pepper. Add the water to make a thick paste. Add a teaspoon of water at a time if you need more. Toss the cut plantains in this mixture to coat evenly.

In a big wok, heat enough oil for deep-frying. Once hot, drop in the plantains carefully. Deep-fry for a few minutes, turning them every now and then. Remove from the oil, drain with a slotted spoon and transfer to a bowl lined with a paper towel. Discard the oil.

For the curry, heat the oil in the same wok, on high heat. Once hot, add the red chilies, mustard and cumin seeds. Once the seeds start to sputter, after a few seconds, add the curry leaves and the green chilies. Reduce heat to medium. When the curry leaves change color, in 30 seconds, add the lentils and split chickpeas. Cook until the split chickpeas are slightly brown, 1 to 2 minutes, on medium heat. Add the soybeans, turmeric, chili powder and cilantro. Simmer on low heat until the soybeans are soft, 4 to 5 minutes. Add the coconut milk and let it take on all the flavors of the spices, around 2 minutes. Add the fried plantains and toss well. Season with salt and pepper. Garnish with cilantro, fresh soybeans and add some avocado slices.

I like to eat this curry just by itself, but you can serve it hot with some plain or cauliflower rice.

We don't really combine vegetables in our dals in North India where I am from. It is something I have learned to do in my time in America and Holland. Both countries have a love for hearty soups. This is a springtime soup for me and has so much freshness hiding in it with the basil and mint. It's a breeze to make and extremely healthy.

GREEN PEA & CHILKA MOONG DAL SOUP

Serves 4

CRUNCHY GREEN PEAS

1 tsp olive oil

1 tbsp (6) cumin seeds

1 cup (145 g) fresh green peas

1 tsp red chili flakes

Salt to taste

SOUP

2 tbsp (30 ml) olive oil

1 onion, chopped

3 cloves garlic, minced

1 tbsp (5 g) coriander powder

½ cup (108 g) split mung beans, with skin on (moong dal)

3 cups (720 ml) vegetable broth

2 cups (290 g) green peas

4 cups (120 g) spinach

1 cup (24 g) basil leaves, loosely packed

½ cup (15 g) mint leaves, loosely packed

Salt and pepper to taste

For the crunchy peas, heat the oil in a pan. Once hot, add the cumin seeds. Once they sputter, after a few seconds, add the peas and cook for a few minutes on high heat until they get crunchy. Add the chili flakes and salt and toss. Set aside.

Heat the oil in a deep pan on high heat. Once hot, add the chopped onion and cook until transparent, 1 to 2 minutes. Add the garlic and coriander and cook for another 2 to 3 minutes or until the raw smell of the garlic is gone. Add the beans and stir to mix well. Add the broth and bring to a boil. Lower the heat and simmer for 15 to 18 minutes or until the beans are cooked and soft.

Add the green peas and cook for around 5 minutes. Add the spinach and stir so you get the spinach to wilt, 1 to 2 minutes. Puree the lentil mix with an immersion blender. Add the basil and mint leaves and puree again. Add salt and pepper to taste and serve hot with the crunchy green peas, basil and mint leaves, melon seeds and a swirl of coconut milk.

Bok choy is such a delicious vegetable and so ubiquitous in Asian cooking. In this dish I have tried to combine my love for those Asian flavors with Indian ones to create this curry. It is a no-fuss dish that strongly delivers on the flavor and is wonderful to dig into on a busy night. It highlights so much veggie goodness teamed up with some soul-comforting legumes.

MISO TURMERIC FLAGEOLET CURRY
with GRILLED BOK CHOY

Serves 4

DRESSING

1 tsp sugar

1 tsp sesame oil

2 tsp (10 ml) soy sauce

FLAGEOLET CURRY

1 tbsp (15 ml) oil

2 shallots, finely chopped

1 tbsp (9 g) black sesame seeds

2 cloves garlic, minced

1" (2.5-cm) piece ginger, grated

2 tsp (10 ml) white miso paste

1⅓ cups (400 g) canned flageolet beans, rinsed

Salt and pepper to taste

1 tbsp (15 ml) oil

3 bok choy, halved

For the dressing, combine the sugar, sesame oil and soy sauce. Mix well and set aside.

For the curry, heat 1 tablespoon (15 ml) of oil in a pan. Once hot, add the shallots and the sesame seeds. Cook until the shallots are transparent, 2 to 3 minutes. Add the garlic and ginger and cook on medium heat until the raw smell of the garlic and ginger is gone, 2 to 3 minutes. Lower the heat to low and then add the miso paste and stir to combine. Add the flageolet beans and stir again to mix everything together. Cook for a few minutes. Add salt and pepper and take off the heat.

Heat the oil in a grill pan on high heat. When hot, add the bok choy cut side down and cook each side for a few minutes each until slightly charred and a little wilted.

To serve, transfer the curry to a flat dish and lay the bok choy on top. Drizzle with the dressing, sesame seeds, cut spring onions and red chili. Serve hot with fried rice.

note: *Dried flageolet beans are easier to find than canned. If you cannot find the canned version, you can use ¾ cup (162 g) of dried beans. Rinse well, barely cover with water and bring to a boil. Reduce the heat to low and simmer, covered, for 50 to 60 minutes until the beans are cooked through but not mushy.*

Dishes with cashew-based sauces are common and popular in India and are used as a base for either meat or vegetarian dishes. I love this dish because the creamy element of the cashew sauce goes so well with the crunchy broccolinis and the nutty and creamy flavor of the urad dal.

URAD DAL & BROCCOLINI STIR-FRY *with* CASHEW SAUCE

Serves 4

BLACK LENTIL FRY
1 cup (216 g) whole black gram beans (whole urad dal), soaked for 12–24 hours

1 tbsp (15 ml) oil

1 tsp fennel seeds

1 red onion, chopped

1 tsp cumin powder

¼ cup (60 ml) water

Salt and pepper to taste

CASHEW SAUCE
¾ cup (92 g) cashews, lightly roasted

2 medium onions, chopped into quarters

3 tbsp (45 ml) tomato paste

¼ cup (60 ml) coconut milk

3–4 cloves garlic

1 tsp garam masala

1 tsp chili powder

¼ tsp turmeric powder

1 tsp coconut sugar

1 tbsp (15 ml) lime juice

Salt and pepper to taste

1 tbsp (15 ml) oil

¼ cup (40 g) raisins, soaked in water

BROCCOLINI FRY
½ lb (225 g) broccolini

1 tbsp (15 ml) oil

2 cloves garlic, sliced

1 tbsp (15 ml) balsamic vinegar

Salt and pepper to taste

Rinse the soaked beans a few times under cold water and drain.

For the black lentil fry, heat the oil in a pan on high heat. Once hot, add the fennel seeds. Once they start to sputter, after a few seconds, add the onion. Lower the heat to medium and cook until the onion is translucent and slightly browned, 5 to 6 minutes. Add the beans and the cumin. Stir to combine. Add the water and simmer, covered, for 30 to 40 minutes. Add the salt and pepper and turn off the heat.

While the beans are cooking, blitz the cashews to a fine powder using a food processor. Add the onions, tomato paste, coconut milk, garlic, garam masala, chili powder, turmeric, coconut sugar, lime juice, salt and pepper and process until everything is combined into a smooth sauce. In a pan, heat the oil. Once hot, add the cashew sauce. Reduce the heat to low and cook the sauce for around 10 minutes. Stir regularly to make sure the sauce doesn't burn. If the mix is too dry add a tablespoon (15 ml) at time of water or coconut milk. Drain the raisins and add to the sauce. Turn off the heat and set aside.

For the broccolini fry, wash and cut off the tough edges of the broccolini. Pat dry. Heat the oil in a flat pan on high heat. Once hot, add the broccolini and fry on high heat for a few minutes, turning and tossing regularly. Add the garlic slices and the balsamic vinegar and continue to cook on high heat for a few more minutes. Add salt and pepper to taste. When the broccolini is slightly charred, it is ready.

To serve, spoon some cashew sauce on a plate and top with a scoop of beans and some broccolini. Sprinkle with roasted pistachio nuts and garnish with a few basil leaves.

This is another curry that incorporates fruit—the apricots provide a refreshing zesty sweet bite to the creaminess of the rest of the dish. This curry inspired by Eastern flavors is always a big hit with anyone who has a love of mild spicy deliciousness with a bit of a twist.

APRICOT BROCCOLI CURRY

Serves 4

ROASTED SPICE MIX
Drop of oil
1 dried red chili
2 tsp (4 g) split chickpeas (chana dal)
1 tsp coriander seeds
¾ tsp poppy seeds
¼ tsp fenugreek seeds
Small piece of cinnamon
1 green cardamom pod
2 whole cloves
2 tsp (3 g) desiccated coconut

CURRY
3 tbsp (45 g) coconut oil, divided
6 apricots, cut in half and pitted
2 shallots, finely chopped
4 cloves garlic, minced
1" (2.5-cm) piece ginger, grated
Salt to taste
1 red bell pepper, cut into chunks
¾ cup (180 ml) coconut milk
2 cups (180 g) broccoli florets
1 tsp lime juice

For the spice mix, heat the drop of oil in a pan on medium heat and dry roast the red chili. Once the chili puffs up, less than a minute, transfer it to a bowl. In the same pan, dry roast the split chickpeas, coriander, poppy seeds, fenugreek, cinnamon, cardamom, cloves and coconut for a minute on medium-high heat or until the spices are fragrant. Keep a close eye on it; you don't want the spices to burn. Transfer all the spices including the dried chili to a spice grinder and grind to a fine powder.

Heat 1 tablespoon (15 g) of coconut oil in a grill pan. Once hot, place the apricots cut side down and grill on medium heat for 2 to 3 minutes on each side until slightly charred. The riper the apricots are, the less time needed. Transfer to a bowl.

In the same pan where you roasted the spices, heat 2 tablespoons (30 g) of coconut oil. Once hot, add the shallots and cook for 2 to 3 minutes or until the shallots are translucent. Then add the garlic, ginger and salt. Cook for an additional 2 minutes or until the raw smell of the garlic and ginger is gone. Add 1½ tablespoons (8 g) of the spice mix and stir for a minute and then add the red bell pepper chunks. Cook on medium-low heat for around 5 minutes before adding the coconut milk. Add the coconut milk and cook for 2 to 3 minutes and then add the broccoli. Simmer on low heat for 10 minutes or until the broccoli is soft and cooked but not mushy. Add the lime juice, stir to mix and add the grilled apricot and toss to mix.

Garnish with toasted cashews and cilantro leaves. Serve hot with jasmine rice.

This dish has the amazing ability to marry two big cultures as if the union had always existed. The Indian flavors and the Asian ones come together in one bite. Like any good lentil dish that uses the split variety of lentils, it is fast and simple to make and delivers hugely with its flavors.

RED CURRY MASOOR DAL

Serves 4

1 cup (192 g) red lentils (split masoor dal)

3 cups (720 ml) water

1 tbsp (15 g) coconut oil

1 tsp cumin seeds

2 medium red onions, chopped fine

1 red chili, chopped

3–4 cloves garlic, minced

1" (2.5-cm) piece ginger, grated

3 tbsp (45 ml) red curry paste

Salt to taste

TEMPERING

2 tbsp (30 g) coconut oil

1 tsp cumin seeds

4–5 cloves garlic, sliced thin

1 tsp red chili powder

Rinse the lentils well and then combine them with the water in a deep pan. Bring to a boil on high heat, removing any foam with a spoon. Reduce the heat to low and cook, covered, for 10 to 12 minutes. Take the lentils off the heat once cooked and set aside. Do not drain.

While the lentils are cooking, heat the oil in a pan on high heat. Once hot, add the cumin seeds, onions, red chili, garlic and ginger. Cook on high heat, while stirring often, until the onions are transparent and the raw smell of the garlic and ginger is gone, 3 to 4 minutes. Reduce the heat to medium low, add the red curry paste and stir often to mix. Cook for 2 to 3 minutes and then add the salt and the cooked dal. Stir to mix the curry paste into the dal and cook for another 5 minutes.

For the tempering, heat the oil in a pan and add the cumin, garlic and chili powder. Cook on medium-high heat and stir continuously. Cook for just a minute and then quickly add the tempering to the lentils, either mixing it in or leaving it as a dollop on top. Garnish with cilantro, cucumber and red chili slices and serve hot with plain white rice.

Enticing Vegan
POWER BOWLS

Indian hospitality is famous, and it is common to be served at least two warm dishes for every meal. These two dishes are usually family favorites or paired dishes that are universally special together. Unlike the previous section where the dish could be potentially eaten all by itself, this section focuses on pairings. They are carefully crafted to maximize the comfort aspect that is so important to wholesome cooking. Served with rice or fresh Indian bread, these meals are lip-smackingly delicious in their simplicity.

These vegan power bowls also celebrate the vibrancy of local produce at hand.

I have put together my favorite combinations in this section with each bowl, but I urge the reader to mix and match elements from different bowls to make their own creations to suit their palate.

One of my mom's favorite things to make was *aloo matar* (potatoes with green peas), because it came together fairly quickly and was really inexpensive to make. Vegetarian food in India contains a fair amount of potatoes with many ways to cook them. So I grew up eating a lot of potatoes. This dish has been my favorite during the years. In this recipe I have combined the peas and potatoes with new favorites, bulgur and asparagus. The toasty vinaigrette binds it all together.

TURMERIC BULGUR LENTILS *with* GREEN PEA POTATOES, GRILLED ASPARAGUS & TAHINI VINAIGRETTE

Serves 4

TAHINI VINAIGRETTE
3 tbsp (45 ml) olive oil
1 tbsp (15 ml) balsamic vinegar
1 tbsp (15 ml) tahini
1 tsp Dijon mustard
1½ tsp (7 ml) agave syrup
1 clove garlic, minced
Pinch of salt

TURMERIC BULGUR LENTILS
¼ cup (50 g) puy lentils, or ½ cup (120 g) canned
2 cups (480 ml) water
½ cup (75 g) bulgur wheat
1 tsp turmeric powder
Juice of ½ lemon
Salt and pepper to taste

GREEN PEAS POTATOES
1 cup (135 g) frozen green peas
1 tbsp (15 ml) olive oil
5 medium potatoes, bite-size cubes
1 tbsp (4 g) fresh thyme
1 tsp mustard seeds
Salt to taste

GRILLED ASPARAGUS
1 tbsp (15 ml) olive oil
10–12 asparagus spears, trimmed and blanched
Salt and pepper to taste

(continued)

TURMERIC BULGUR LENTILS *with* GREEN PEA POTATOES, GRILLED ASPARAGUS & TAHINI VINAIGRETTE (cont.)

For the vinaigrette, mix the oil, vinegar, tahini, mustard, agave, garlic and salt together in a small dish and mix until fully combined. Keep excess in a sealed container in the refrigerator for up to 3 days.

Rinse the lentils and combine them in a pan with the water. Bring to a boil on high heat and then lower the heat and simmer, covered, for 20 to 25 minutes. Once the lentils are soft, drain any excess water. If using canned lentils, rinse and drain before using.

Make the bulgur according to the instructions on the package, adding the turmeric to the water you use to cook the bulgur. Once ready, drain the excess water and combine with the cooked lentils. Add the lemon juice, salt and pepper and mix well.

Place the frozen green peas in a bowl with just enough water to cover them, and leave to thaw for a few minutes. Skip this step if using fresh peas.

For the green peas and potatoes, heat the oil in a pan. Once hot, add the potatoes with the thyme and mustard seeds. Cook the potatoes on medium heat, stirring often, making sure they don't get burnt. Once the potatoes are nice and brown, 10 to 15 minutes, turn the heat to low. Drain the green peas and add to the potatoes. Cook on low heat for about 5 minutes and season with salt.

Heat the olive oil in a pan over medium heat. Add the asparagus in a single layer on the pan. Evenly distribute salt and pepper over the asparagus. Cook the asparagus until crisp-tender and slightly browned, 3 to 4 minutes, occasionally turning the spears to brown all sides.

To serve, place the turmeric bulgur lentils in a large bowl and top with the masala green peas potatoes and the grilled asparagus. Drizzle with the tahini vinaigrette and garnish with kiwi, pomegranate arils and micro greens.

note: I always prepare my potatoes without cooking them in water first. If you want this part of the preparation to go slightly faster, cook the potatoes in water for 4 to 5 minutes before cooking them in oil. Reduce the cooking time in oil and spices to 2 to 3 minutes.

I used to watch my mom make dal dumplings as a kid. I remember her telling me how to whip the lentils so as to make them super fluffy, light and with a melt-in-your-mouth texture. I watched her whip the lentil mix with her fingers and was always fascinated with how she got them to be so good. I have never been more proud when years later I tried them on my own and got them right. Contrary to how I remember it, the process of making these is super easy. Adding the dal in this curry, in a different form, tasted just out of this world.

SPINACH CURRY *with* DAL DUMPLINGS

Serves 4 with extra dumplings

TAMARIND CHUTNEY
5 tbsp (75 ml) tamarind paste

½ cup (120 ml) water

1 tsp cumin powder

1 tsp ginger powder

¼ tsp chili powder

5 tbsp (70 g) jaggery

URAD DAL DUMPLINGS
½ cup (108 g) white lentils (split and dehusked urad dal), soaked for 3–4 hours

½ cup (96 g) split pigeon peas (toor dal), soaked for 3–4 hours

1 tbsp (12 g) split green peas, soaked for 3–4 hours

¼ cup (60 ml) water

1" (2.5-cm) piece ginger

1 tsp roasted cumin powder

1 tbsp (1 g) cilantro, chopped

Pinch of asafetida

Salt

¼ tsp baking soda

SPINACH CURRY
1 lb (454 g) spinach

3–4 tbsp (45–60 ml) oil

1 tsp cumin seeds

1 green chili, chopped

3–4 cloves garlic, minced

1" (2.5-cm) piece ginger, grated

½ tsp chili powder

½ tsp turmeric powder

½ tsp cumin powder

1 tsp coriander powder

1 tsp jaggery (add more if your green chili is very hot)

¼ cup (60 ml) coconut milk

Oil for deep-frying

(continued)

SPINACH CURRY *with* DAL DUMPLINGS (cont.)

Combine the tamarind paste and the water in a pan and mix together on low heat. Add the cumin, ginger, chili powder and jaggery and simmer for 8 to 10 minutes, stirring often. Set aside to cool.

For the dal dumplings, rinse all the white lentils, split pigeon peas and split green peas in cold water and drain. Grind them in a food processor with the water until it is a fine paste. You should feel no sandy texture if you rub the mixture between two fingers. Transfer to a bowl. Add the ginger, cumin, cilantro, asafetida and salt to the lentil batter and stir vigorously for a few minutes to aerate the mix. Add the baking soda and stir vigorously again.

Boil water, add the spinach and cook for 2 to 3 minutes. Drain immediately and rinse with cold water to stop the cooking process. Puree the spinach to a smooth paste in a food processor and set aside.

For the curry, heat the oil in a pan on high heat. Once hot, add the cumin seeds. Once they sputter, after a few seconds, add the green chili, garlic and ginger. Cook until the raw smell of the ginger and garlic is gone, 2 to 3 minutes. Now add the chili powder, turmeric, cumin, coriander and jaggery and cook for another 3 to 4 minutes. Add in the pureed spinach and cook for 6 to 8 minutes. Add the coconut milk, and let gently simmer for 3 to 4 minutes on low heat. Turn off the heat.

In a pan, heat enough oil for deep-frying on high heat. Once the oil is hot—test this by dropping a little of the lentil mix into the oil; if it floats to the top, the oil is ready—take a tablespoonful (15 ml) at a time of the lentil mix and drop into the oil. Don't overcrowd, as the dumplings will get stuck to each other. Fry each side for a few minutes. The dumplings should be light brown in color. Drain any excess oil and transfer to a bowl lined with a kitchen towel. Repeat with all the batter.

Add the fried dumplings to the spinach curry and toss slightly to combine. Serve hot with the tamarind chutney, and some millet and steamed carrots on the side. Garnish with cilantro, baby spinach leaves and sliced onion.

note: I like to make a lot of dumplings just to snack on, and this recipe will make a lot of extras. If you only want enough for 4, halve the recipe for the dumplings.

This stew is inspired by a dal dish in India that is meant to be sour and sweet. It is also, in part, inspired by a North African chickpea stew. I loved combining these two delicious recipes into one. The chickpeas are mild and the vegetables surprise with a sweet and spicy touch.

CHICKPEA DAL STEW with JAGGERY & HARISSA VEGETABLES

Serves 4

½ cup (100 g) dry chickpeas (chana dal), soaked overnight

½ cup (102 g) split pigeon peas (toor dal)

¼ cup (50 g) split red lentils (split masoor dal)

5 cups (1.2 L) water, divided

JAGGERY & HARISSA VEGETABLES
2 tsp (10 ml) harissa paste

1 tsp tamarind paste

2 tsp (10 ml) water

4 tbsp (60 ml) olive oil

Pinch of asafetida

2 tsp (6 g) mustard seeds

2 whole cloves

1 dried red chili, broken into 2–3 pieces

1 tsp red chili powder

1 plantain, peeled, sliced into angled slices and parboiled for 6 minutes

2 cups (280 g) peeled and cubed butternut squash, parboiled for 6 minutes

1 eggplant, cut into large cubes

4 tbsp (56 g) jaggery

CHICKPEA DAL STEW
2 tbsp (30 ml) olive oil

2 tsp (4 g) cumin seeds

1 onion, chopped

2 cloves garlic, minced

1 tsp paprika powder

2 medium tomatoes, chopped

Rinse the chickpeas, pigeon peas and the lentils separately. In one pot add the split pigeon peas and the lentils with 3 cups (720 ml) of water and in the second pot combine the chickpeas with 2 cups (480 ml) of water. Bring both pots to a boil. Lower the heat and cook, covered, 20 to 25 minutes for the lentils and 30 to 35 minutes for the chickpeas. Once done, turn off the heat and do not drain.

Mix together the harissa paste, tamarind paste and water and set aside.

For the vegetables, heat the oil in a pan on high heat. Once hot, add the asafetida. After 30 seconds add the mustard seeds and the cloves. Once the mustard seeds sputter, after a few seconds, add the red chili and red chili powder. Stir to mix well and cook for a minute or two until the oil gets infused with the spices. Add the plantain and cook for 5 to 6 minutes. Add the butternut squash and cook again for 5 to 6 minutes. Add the eggplant last with the harissa and tamarind paste. Toss the vegetables and continue to cook for 6 to 8 minutes or until the eggplant is soft. Add the jaggery, stir and cook for 5 to 8 minutes. Turn off the heat.

Heat the oil for the chickpea dal stew on high heat. Once hot, add the cumin seeds. Once they sputter, in a few seconds, add the onion and the garlic. Lower the heat to medium and cook until the onion is soft and transparent and the raw smell of the garlic is gone, 3 to 4 minutes. Add the paprika and stir well to mix. Add the tomatoes and cook for 3 to 4 minutes or until the tomatoes are soft. Add the chickpeas with their cooking liquid. Lower the heat to medium-low and simmer for 10 minutes. Add the cooked pigeon peas and lentils and simmer again for around 15 minutes on low heat. Turn off the heat.

Serve hot with the jaggery and harissa vegetables and cooked couscous on the side. Garnish with cilantro, micro greens and some roasted pine nuts.

I often joke about how I Indianize everything I lay my hands on. I have always loved this Italian soup, which has been successfully turned Indian in my opinion. Unlike the other vegan bowls here, the pairing of ingredients happens in one pot. It has a mild flavor and is extremely healthy with all the protein that goes into this soup. The fresh bread works flawlessly in its role in scooping up the inviting meal.

DAL MINESTRONE

Serves 4

1 cup (200 g) chickpeas, soaked overnight and drained

1 cup (185 g) red kidney beans, soaked overnight and drained

½ cup (96 g) brown lentils (whole masoor dal), soaked overnight

8 cups (2 L) water, divided

4 tbsp (60 ml) olive oil

2 medium onions, chopped

8–10 cloves garlic, crushed

2 tsp (6 g) turmeric powder

1 tsp red chili powder

2 cups (200 g) chopped celery

1 beetroot, chopped in small cubes

Salt and pepper to taste

1 cup (30 g) loosely packed mint, chopped

1 cup (60 g) loosely packed parsley, chopped

1 cup (16 g) loosely packed cilantro, chopped

Rinse the chickpeas, kidney beans and lentils under cold water a few times. Combine the chickpeas with 2 cups (480 ml) of water and bring to a boil. In a separate pot, combine the kidney beans with 2 cups (480 ml) of water and bring to a boil. In a third pot, combine the lentils with 2 cups (480 ml) of water and bring to a boil. Reduce the heat for all three and simmer with the lid on 20 to 25 minutes for the chickpeas and the lentils. They should be cooked through but still firm, not mushy. Simmer for 1 to 2 hours for the kidney beans, until cooked through but not mushy. Drain all three when done and set aside.

In a large pan, heat the oil on high heat. Once hot, add the onions and cook on low heat until they are soft and transparent, 8 to 10 minutes. Add the garlic, raise the heat to medium and cook until the raw smell of the garlic is gone, 3 to 4 minutes. Add the turmeric and chili powder and stir to mix it all in. Add the celery and the beetroot and stir to mix well. Cook for 15 minutes, stirring often. Add salt, mint, parsley and cilantro. Cook while stirring for a few minutes.

Add the chickpeas and the kidney beans to the onion mixture. Stir everything to combine and cook for a few minutes. Add the cooked lentils and 2 cups (480 ml) of water and simmer for 20 to 25 minutes. Once the chickpeas, kidney beans and lentils are heated, turn off the heat and add more salt and pepper if required. Divide minestrone between bowls, garnish with chopped parsley and spring onions and serve hot with fresh bread.

note: The beans can be cooked and prepped the day before or on weekends. To determine if the beans are cooked, take one and press it between your thumb and forefinger. If the bean collapses easily, it is cooked.

What I really love about this dal is that you can combine any nine lentils together. Every time I make this dal, it comes out slightly different. I never use the same combination, and you shouldn't either. A bowlful of this concoction, packed with nine different lentils full of proteins, fiber and folic acid is incredibly healthy. The slightly smooth yet textured lentils are combined with the crunchy, nutty dukkah asparagus.

NINE LENTILS DAL *with* DUKKAH ASPARAGUS

Serves 4

DUKKAH
½ tsp pine nuts
1 tbsp (8 g) pistachios
1 tbsp (9 g) sunflower seeds
¼ cup (33 g) hazelnuts
1 tbsp (8 g) almonds
½ tsp fennel seeds
1½ tbsp (7 g) coriander seeds
1½ tbsp (14 g) white sesame seeds
1 tbsp (9 g) black sesame seeds
1 tbsp (6 g) cumin seeds
½ tbsp (4 g) paprika powder
½ tsp sea salt

NINE LENTILS DAL
1 tbsp (13 g) dry navy beans
2 tbsp (25 g) chickpeas
2 tbsp (25 g) black chickpeas (chana dal)
2 tbsp (25 g) black-eyed peas (lobia)
1 tbsp (14 g) split and dehusked mung beans (split and dehusked moong dal)
1 tbsp (14 g) black beans
1 tbsp (13 g) split chickpeas (chana dal)
1 tbsp (13 g) split pigeon peas (toor dal)
2½ cups (600 ml) water
(Soak all lentils for 2 hours if using a pressure cooker. If not, soak overnight.)

3 tbsp (45 ml) oil
1 tsp cumin seeds
1 tsp carom seeds
2 medium onions, chopped
1"(2.5-cm) piece ginger, grated
4–5 cloves garlic, minced
2 medium tomatoes, chopped
1 tbsp (15 ml) tomato paste
1 tbsp (5 g) coriander powder
½ tsp red chili powder
½ tsp turmeric powder
Salt to taste
½ tsp garam masala

DUKKAH ASPARAGUS
1 tbsp (15 ml) oil
3 cups (400 g) asparagus tips
2 cloves garlic, thinly sliced
Sea salt to taste

(continued)

For the dukkah, dry roast the pine nuts, pistachios, sunflower seeds, hazelnuts and almonds in a pan on medium heat, 2 to 3 minutes, until only slightly browned. Transfer to a food processor and pulse to a rough mix. Don't overmix. You don't want a fine powder. Gently roast the fennel seeds, coriander seeds, white and black sesame seeds and cumin, around 2 minutes. Add the spices to the nut mix and pulse a few times. Add the paprika and salt to the rest of the ingredients and stir to mix in. Transfer to a jar.

Rinse all the beans, peas and lentils. Transfer to a pressure cooker (if using) and add the water. Give the legumes 6 or 7 whistles on high heat. Lower the heat to low and simmer for 20 minutes. Turn off the heat and release the pressure.

If not using a pressure cooker, transfer the beans, peas and lentils to a deep pan with the water and bring to a boil on high heat. Lower the heat to low and cover. Simmer for 40 to 50 minutes until all the beans are cooked. Do not drain.

Heat the oil in a pan on high heat. Once hot, add the cumin and carom seeds. Once they sputter, after a few seconds, add the onions and cook until the onions are translucent, about a minute. Add the ginger and garlic. Lower the heat to medium and cook until the onions begin to brown and the raw smell of the ginger and garlic is gone, 3 to 4 minutes. Add the chopped tomatoes and the tomato paste. Stir to combine and cook until the tomatoes are mushy, 4 to 5 minutes. Add the coriander, red chili and turmeric. Stir again to mix and cook for a few minutes. Add the cooked lentils and season with salt. Simmer for 10 to 12 minutes on low heat, stirring occasionally. Add the garam masala, stir in and turn off the heat.

For the asparagus, heat the oil in a pan on high heat. Once hot, add the asparagus and fry for 2 to 3 minutes, turning constantly. Add the sliced garlic and salt right at the end. Take off the heat as soon as the asparagus starts to char just a little.

Serve the lentils on a bed of basmati rice, topped with the asparagus. Sprinkle 2 tablespoons (12 g) of dukkah generously on top and garnish with cilantro, grapes, cucumber and cherry tomatoes.

I love artichokes. It's my soul vegetable. If I could be a vegetable, it would definitely be the artichoke. It can be a daunting vegetable to prepare, but once you do, you wonder why you hadn't been doing it every other day. It's also a vegetable that is tedious to prepare for just a tiny bit of flesh on the inside. But it is so worth it! It is made very simply in this recipe and is deliciously paired with vaal (butter beans). Another addition is the highly popular salad in India called *kachumbar*. This chopped salad adds crunch to the dish. The Indianized chimichurri sauce just brings all elements together with all its tanginess. This meal can be eaten cold or warm and works great as lunch or dinner prepared ahead of time.

VAAL DAL *with* KACHUMBAR SALAD, POPPY SEED ARTICHOKES & CHIMICHURRI SAUCE

Serves 4 to 6

POPPY SEED ARTICHOKE
3 green artichokes
3 tsp (15 ml) lemon juice
Olive oil
6 cloves garlic
Salt and pepper
3 tsp (9 g) poppy seeds

CHILI QUINOA RICE
1 cup (170 g) quinoa
1½ cups (280 g) cooked rice
1 green chili, chopped

CHIMICHURRI SAUCE
1 cup (16 g) cilantro, packed
½ cup (120 ml) olive oil
1 red chili
2 tbsp (30 ml) red wine vinegar
1 tsp sea salt
Pepper to taste

BUTTER BEANS WITH KACHUMBAR SALAD
3⅓ cups (800 g) canned butter beans (vaal dal)
1 tbsp (15 ml) oil
2 tsp (4 g) cumin powder
1 tsp fennel seeds
Salt and pepper to taste
1¼ cups (165 g) cubed cucumber
8–10 sun-dried tomatoes, sliced
8–10 radishes, finely chopped
1 red onion, finely chopped
8–10 ground cherries, quartered
1 tsp lemon juice

(continued)

VAAL DAL *with* KACHUMBAR SALAD, POPPY SEED ARTICHOKES *&* CHIMICHURRI SAUCE (cont.)

Preheat the oven to 400°F (205°C).

To clean the artichokes, cut off the stalk and peel off the tough outer layers. When you reach the softer layer, use a serrated knife to cut off about ¾ inch (2 cm) from the top. Cut the artichoke in half and use a spoon to remove the hairy part. Quickly apply some lemon juice to prevent discoloring. Place each half of an artichoke on a piece of aluminum foil on a baking sheet. Drizzle generously with olive oil, place one clove of garlic in each artichoke, and add the salt, pepper and poppy seeds. Fold the foil around the artichokes and bake in the oven for around 40 minutes. The artichokes should be melt-in-your-mouth soft at this stage.

While the artichokes are cooking, prepare the quinoa according to the package instructions. Once cooked, add in the rice and mix. Sprinkle the chopped chili on top, cover and set aside.

Once the artichokes are done, turn off the oven, remove the artichokes and carefully open the foil and remove the garlic (for the chimichurri sauce). Fold the foil back and pop into the turned-off oven to stay warm.

For the chimichurri sauce, combine the roasted garlic, cilantro, oil, chili, vinegar, salt and pepper in a food processor and blitz until everything is combined. Transfer to a bowl and set aside.

Rinse and drain the butter beans. In a pan, heat the oil on high heat. Once hot, add the cumin and fennel seeds. Once they sputter, after a few seconds, add the butter beans. Toss to combine all elements. Lower heat to medium, add salt and pepper and cook for 4 to 5 minutes. Turn off the heat.

In a bowl, combine the butter beans with the cucumber, tomatoes, radishes, onion and ground cherries. Drizzle with lemon juice and toss to mix.

Serve hot with a scoop of the butter bean mix in a bowl, with chili quinoa and artichoke. Drizzle with the chimichurri sauce and garnish with cilantro and some chopped red onion.

note: When you buy artichokes, buy the green ones that feel somewhat soft in general. The ones that are drying out will not have as much meat on the inside and it will be tough to remove the dry outer layers.

This curry and this bowl are made up of everyday recipes from my mom's kitchen. I don't ever remember her using dried green peas but they are delicious and once cooked offer a surprisingly creamy texture. The bell peppers and potatoes give body to the curry and add a lot of flavor. With the ginger cauliflower, this bowl is quite complete for me.

DRIED GREEN PEAS, POTATO & PEPPER CURRY *with* GINGER CAULIFLOWER

Serves 4 to 6

1 cup (200 g) dried green peas

½ cup (108 g) black beans

3 cups (720 ml) water

(Soak the peas and beans for 3–4 hours if using a pressure cooker. If not, soak for at least 7–8 hours.)

3 tbsp (45 ml) oil

1 tsp cumin seeds

2 red onions, chopped

1" (2.5-cm) piece ginger, grated

4–5 cloves garlic, minced

2 cups (300 g) square-cut red and green bell peppers

3 small potatoes, cut into cubes

1 tbsp (8 g) Curry Powder (page 39)

½ tsp turmeric powder

1 tbsp (5 g) coriander powder

½ tsp red chili powder

½ tsp sea salt

GINGER CAULIFLOWER

2 tbsp (30 ml) oil

1 onion, sliced

2" (5-cm) piece ginger, julienned

4 cups (400 g) cauliflower florets

1 tsp turmeric powder

Salt to taste

Rinse the dried green peas and beans. Transfer to a pressure cooker and combine with the water. On high heat give 5 to 6 whistles and then lower the heat and simmer for around 20 minutes. Release the pressure and set aside. Do not drain.

If not using a pressure cooker, transfer the peas and beans to a pot and combine with the water. Bring to a boil and remove any foam with a spoon. Lower the heat to low and simmer, covered, for 40 to 45 minutes or until the peas and beans are soft and cooked through. Do not drain.

Heat the oil in a deep pan on high heat. Once hot, add the cumin seeds. Once the cumin sputters, after a few seconds, add the onions, ginger and garlic. Lower the heat to medium and cook until the onions start to brown a little and the raw smell of the ginger and garlic is gone, 2 to 3 minutes.

Add the bell peppers, potatoes, curry powder, turmeric, coriander, chili powder and salt. Stir well to combine and cook for 2 to 3 minutes until the spices are fragrant.

Add the cooked green peas and bean mix and stir again to combine all the ingredients. Simmer on low heat for around 20 minutes.

While the curry is cooking, make the ginger cauliflower. In a wok, heat the oil on high heat. Once hot, add the onion and ginger. While stirring often, cook until the onion is browning and the raw smell of the ginger is gone, 3 to 4 minutes. Add the cauliflower florets and stir to combine. Add the turmeric and toss. Cook on medium heat for 8 to 10 minutes, stirring regularly to make sure the cauliflower doesn't burn. Add a tablespoon (15 ml) of water at a time if the cauliflower sticks to the wok. Once the cauliflower looks charred a little, add salt, mix well and take off the heat.

Serve on a bed of brown basmati rice, topped with a generous scoop of the curry with the ginger cauliflower. Garnish with sliced radish, chopped cilantro and some shredded red cabbage on the side.

This dish is inspired by *erwtensoep,* or split green pea soup, in Holland. It is a time-tested popular dish here because it's a meal in itself. It is easy, healthy and most of all convenient. The Dutch version includes meat, as much of their dishes do, with the addition of winter vegetables. The split green pea was never used in our house and giving the Dutch soup an Indian version was exciting. It's a soup with heart and certainly not for the fainthearted. You don't really need anything else for hours if you eat this. It makes for a great dinner meal and is cozy, healthy and comforting.

SPLIT GREEN PEAS *with* VEGETABLE CHIPS & PINEAPPLE CHUTNEY

Serves 4 to 6

VEGETABLE CHIPS
1 beetroot
2 carrots
1 tsp olive oil
Salt and pepper to taste

ROASTED SPICE MIX
½ tbsp (5 g) sesame seeds
Drop of oil
2 tbsp (10 g) coriander seeds
½ tsp cumin seeds
1 red chili
¼ tsp clove powder
1 bay leaf
½ star anise
Pinch of asafetida
½ tsp Himalayan rock salt
½ tsp black pepper
½ tsp turmeric powder

PINEAPPLE CHUTNEY
½ pineapple, cut into very small cubes
1 tsp pumpkin spice
3 tbsp (45 ml) white wine vinegar
½ cup (120 ml) water
½ tsp turmeric powder
¼ tsp red chili powder
2 tbsp (26 g) sugar (add more if your pineapple is not too sweet)

SPLIT MOONG DAL
1 cup (200 g) split green peas, soaked for 2–3 hours
3 cups (720 ml) water
2 tbsp (30 ml) oil
2 onions, chopped
2 carrots, chopped
2 ribs celery, chopped
2 parsnips, chopped
1 leek, sliced in half rounds
Salt and pepper to taste

(continued)

SPLIT GREEN PEAS *with* VEGETABLE CHIPS
& PINEAPPLE CHUTNEY (cont.)

Preheat the oven to 375°F (191°C). Line a baking sheet with parchment paper.

For the vegetable chips, cut the beetroot and the carrots into thin slices with a mandoline and toss them with the oil, salt and pepper. Line the sliced vegetables on the baking sheet, avoiding overlap. Bake for 10 minutes and then flip and bake for another 10 minutes or until the slices are slightly browned but not burnt. Set aside to cool.

While your chips are baking, prepare the spice mix by dry roasting the sesame seeds for a few minutes in a pan on medium heat or until the seeds turn only slightly brown. Watch carefully, as they burn quickly. Transfer to a spice grinder and grind to a fine powder. In the same pan, add a drop of oil and roast the coriander, cumin, chili, clove powder, bay leaf, star anise, asafetida and the rock salt for just a minute until the spices are fragrant. Grind to a fine powder in a spice grinder. Mix in the black pepper and turmeric powder; mix all the ingredients together and set aside.

For the chutney, add the pineapple, pumpkin spice, vinegar, water, turmeric and chili powder in a pan and bring to a boil on high heat. Lower the heat, and then simmer for 20 to 30 minutes until the pineapple is completely cooked through and has taken on the flavors of all the other ingredients. Add the sugar halfway through the cooking process. When the pineapple is completely mushy, remove from the heat and allow to cool.

Rinse the soaked beans and transfer to a pot with the water. Bring to a boil. Remove any foam with a spoon. Lower the heat and simmer, covered, for 20 to 25 minutes. Do not drain.

In another deep pan, heat the oil on high heat. Once hot, lower the heat to medium, add onions and cook until the onions are transparent and soft, 3 to 4 minutes. Add 2 tablespoons (30 g) of the roasted spice mix. Stir to combine with the onions. Cook until the spices are fragrant, around 2 minutes. Add the carrots, celery and parsnips and cook for around 5 minutes, stirring regularly. Add the sliced leek and cook for another 5 minutes, stirring regularly.

Add the beans with their cooking liquid, lower the heat to low and simmer with the lid on for 15 to 18 minutes or until everything is cooked through. Add salt and pepper and turn off the heat.

Serve the split green pea dal hot, topped with the beet and carrot chips and the pineapple chutney on the side.

note: Leftover spices will keep in an airtight container for a few weeks.

As a vegetarian, we eat a lot of potatoes in India but somehow sweet potato never made the cut. I do see it from time to time as popular street food, but it was never used at home. Now, I love sweet potato in a curry when it is introduced to spices. It takes on this creamy, velvety texture and combined with all the spices, it is quite a treat. Here, I have matched some zucchini fries with the sweet potato curry to help balance the flavors, tempering the spiciness of the potatoes.

SPICY SWEET POTATO CURRY *with* ZUCCHINI FRIES

Serves 4 to 6

SPICE MIX
2 dried red chilies
1 tbsp (6 g) fennel seeds
1 tbsp (7 g) coriander seeds
1 tsp caraway seeds
1 tsp cumin seeds
1 black cardamom pod
1 green cardamom pod
¼ tsp black peppercorns
4 whole cloves
½ tbsp (4 g) ginger powder
1 tsp water

1¾ lbs (790 g) sweet potatoes, cut into large chunks
¼ cup + 2 tsp (70 ml) oil, divided

ZUCCHINI FRIES
1 zucchini
¼ cup (23 g) chickpea flour (besan)
½ tsp chili powder
½ tsp turmeric powder
1 tsp cumin powder
2 tbsp (30 ml) almond milk
1–2 tbsp (15–30 ml) water
Salt and pepper to taste

SWEET POTATO CURRY
2 tsp (5 g) Kashmiri chili powder
4 tbsp (60 ml) tomato paste
1 tbsp (13 g) coconut sugar
½ cup (120 ml) water
½ cup (120 ml) coconut milk
Salt to taste

(continued)

SPICY SWEET POTATO CURRY *with* ZUCCHINI FRIES (cont.)

Preheat the oven to 425°F (218°C).

For the spice mix, dry roast the chilies, fennel, coriander, caraway, cumin, black and green cardamom, peppercorns and cloves in a pan on high heat for just a minute. Turn off the heat and transfer to a spice grinder. Grind the spices to a fine powder. Mix in the ginger powder. Add the water, mix well and set aside.

Peel the sweet potatoes and cut them into large chunks. Transfer them to a large pot and add enough water to cover the potatoes. Bring to a boil and cook for 4 to 5 minutes. The potatoes will be half cooked at this point. Drain immediately and run under cold water to stop the cooking process. Once the potatoes are cool, jab each chunk a few times with a fork. In a deep pan, add ¼ cup (60 ml) of oil and fry the potatoes until they turn a little brown around the edges, 8 to 10 minutes. Transfer to a plate lined with kitchen towels.

For the zucchini fries, cut the ends off the zucchini and cut it into strips about 2 to 3 inches (5 to 8 cm) long and ⅓ inch (8 mm) thick. Combine the chickpea flour, chili powder, turmeric, cumin, almond milk, water, salt and pepper and toss the zucchini to coat it well with the ingredients. Place the zucchini strips on a baking tray with space between each strip. Bake for 10 to 15 minutes or until the strips are lightly browned and crunchy.

For the curry, in the same pan that you fried the sweet potatoes, heat the remaining 2 teaspoons (10 ml) of the oil. Add 3 tablespoons (45 g) of the roasted spice mix and the Kashmiri chili powder and stir into the oil for a minute or two. Add the tomato paste and coconut sugar. Stir to mix before adding the sweet potato chunks. Toss the potatoes with the spices and add the water and coconut milk. Cover the pan and on low heat simmer and cook the curry for 10 to 12 minutes or until the potatoes are completely done. Season with salt if needed.

Serve hot with pearl couscous and zucchini fries. Garnish with some greens, cherry tomatoes and cucumber.

note: If your dried chilies are too hot, you can leave them out altogether and increase the Kashmiri chili powder by an additional teaspoon. If your curry still turns out too hot for your taste buds, add a little more sugar and coconut milk.

Okra is my all-time favorite curry. If a stranger offered me okra I'd probably walk off with them! It's all those memories of it in India while growing up that make okra very dear to me. I loved it so much as a child that I would eat everything on my plate and leave it for last, so I could savor every little piece that went into my mouth. This dish is soaked in oil and tomatoes and is an ode to my memories. I combined them with my Italian-inspired thyme potatoes that go quite brilliantly with the tangy okra. Eat with some Indian garlic naan, and you'll be in vegetarian heaven.

OKRA TOMATO CURRY *with* THYME POTATO WEDGES

Serves 4

THYME POTATOES

1 tbsp (15 ml) oil

1 tsp cumin seeds

1 lb (454 g) potatoes, cut into wedges

1 tbsp (4 g) fresh thyme

1 onion, sliced

Salt and pepper to taste

OKRA CURRY

½ cup (120 ml) oil

1 lb (454 g) okra, each cut roughly into 2 pieces

3 medium onions, chopped fine

4–5 cloves garlic, minced

1" (2.5-cm) piece ginger, grated

1 green chili, chopped

2 large tomatoes, chopped

1 tbsp (15 ml) tomato paste

1 tsp coriander powder

½ tsp cumin powder

Salt to taste

For the thyme potatoes, heat the oil in a pan on medium-high heat. Once hot, add the cumin seeds. When the seeds start to sputter, add the potatoes. Cook the potatoes for 20 to 25 minutes on low heat while stirring often, making sure the potatoes don't burn. Halfway through, add the thyme. At the very end, add the onion and cook for another 5 minutes. Season with salt and pepper.

Heat the oil for the okra curry in a deep pan on high heat. While the oil gets hot, wash the okra and dry well. Cut off the head and the tips and cut each pod into 2 pieces. The really small ones you can leave as 1 piece. Once the oil is hot, shallow fry the okra for 3 to 4 minutes. Make sure you stir often. Don't let the okra char or go dark. Transfer the fried okra to a dish lined with kitchen towels.

In the same pan that you fried the okra, on medium heat, add the chopped onions and cook for 8 to 10 minutes or until the onions are browning nicely. Add the garlic, ginger and the chili and cook for another 3 to 4 minutes or until the raw smell of the garlic and ginger is gone. Lower the heat to low and add the tomatoes and tomato paste, stirring to combine everything. Cook until the tomatoes are mushy and somewhat cooked, 5 to 6 minutes. Add the coriander and cumin and stir to combine. Cook for 2 to 3 minutes. Add the okra and stir to mix. Simmer for 15 to 18 minutes or until the okra is cooked through. Right at the end, add the salt.

Divide the okra and the thyme potatoes into bowls. Garnish with red onion, cherry tomatoes and some additional thyme stalks. Serve with garlic naan.

Apart from Indian food, I love Asian flavors, especially from Thailand. I was afraid as I tested this recipe of what the cardamom might do to the flavors. I was prepared to be disappointed. But after a few iterations, I was shocked at how well the cardamom liked being with the other Asian flavors. It gave a nuance I had not expected and gave me a wonderful and warm feeling of familiarity. This is a light, airy curry and when you make this and eat it, you will want to come back to it again and again.

ASPARAGUS & GREEN PEAS CARDAMOM CURRY with GARLICKY CARROTS & SUGAR SNAP PEAS

Serves 4

ASPARAGUS CURRY

1 tbsp (15 g) coconut oil

3 shallots, chopped fine

4–5 cloves garlic, minced

1" (2.5-cm) piece ginger, grated

1 stalk lemongrass, chopped

1 red chili

1½ tsp (7 g) brown sugar

5 green cardamom pods, crushed

6½ tbsp (100 ml) coconut milk, divided

½ lb (225 g) asparagus, trimmed and halved if overlong

1 cup (145 g) fresh green peas

½ tbsp (7 ml) lemon juice

½ cup (120 ml) water

Salt to taste

GARLICKY CARROTS & SUGAR SNAP PEAS

1 tbsp (15 ml) oil

8–10 cloves garlic, sliced

2 carrots, chopped

½ lb (225 g) sugar snap peas, blanched for 3–4 minutes

Salt to taste

For the asparagus curry, heat the oil in a pan. Once hot, add the chopped shallots, garlic and ginger. Cook on medium-low heat for 3 to 4 minutes or until the shallots are translucent and the raw smell of the garlic and ginger is gone. Add the chopped lemongrass, red chili, brown sugar, cardamom and half of the coconut milk. Stir well to combine all the elements and cook for 3 to 4 minutes. Add the asparagus and cook for around 5 minutes. Add the green peas, the remaining coconut milk, lemon juice and water. Simmer for 10 to 15 minutes. Add the salt and turn off the heat.

For the garlicky carrots and sugar snap peas, heat the oil in a pan. Once hot, add the garlic slices and immediately add the carrots. Cook for a few minutes on medium heat or until the carrots are softened slightly. Add the sugar snap peas and cook for 8 to 10 minutes on low heat until the carrots are cooked. Add the salt and turn off the heat.

Serve hot with jasmine rice. Garnish with chopped red chilies, almond slices, cucumber and cilantro.

note: *If using frozen green peas, soak them in warm water to thaw until you need to add them into the curry.*

"Green apple? With potatoes? You must be mad," said my baby girl. Not quite. A curry popular in Sri Lanka is the inspiration for this dish. It is sweet and tangy and the spicy, crunchy green beans make it the perfect combination.

GREEN APPLE & POTATO CURRY
with CRUNCHY GREEN BEANS

Serves 4

APPLE POTATO CURRY
3 tbsp (45 ml) oil
Pinch of asafetida
1 medium onion, finely chopped
1 green chili, chopped
2 cloves garlic, minced
½"(13-mm) piece ginger, grated
2 tbsp (16 g) Curry Powder (page 39)
3 medium skin-on potatoes, cubed
2 green apples, cored and cubed
½ cup (120 ml) water
1 tbsp (14 g) brown sugar
Salt to taste

SPICY GREEN BEANS
3 tbsp (45 ml) oil
Pinch of asafetida
2 tsp (4 g) cumin seeds
1 tsp mustard seeds
2–3 dried red chilies
1 lb (454 g) green beans, cut lengthwise
2 tsp (5 g) coriander powder
1 tsp Kashmiri chili powder
½ tsp turmeric powder
1 tsp amchoor powder
Salt to taste
½ cup (80 g) raisins

BROAD BEANS
2 cups (300 g) raw broad beans (fava beans)
½ tsp nigella seeds (kalonji)

For the apple potato curry, heat the oil in a pan on medium heat. Once hot, add the asafetida and cook for just around 30 seconds. Add the onion, green chili, garlic and ginger and cook until the onion is translucent and the raw smell of the garlic and ginger is gone, around 3 to 4 minutes. Add the curry powder and stir to mix well. Cook for 2 minutes. Add the potatoes and lower the heat to low. Cover the pan and simmer for 8 to 10 minutes, stirring every now and then. Add the apples and cook for another 10 minutes or until the potatoes and apple are somewhat soft. Add the water and brown sugar and simmer for another 30 minutes or until the potatoes and apples are cooked through. Add the salt and turn off the heat.

For the green beans, heat the oil in a pan on medium heat. Once hot, add the asafetida and cook for just 30 seconds. Add the cumin and mustard seeds. Once the seeds start to sputter, after a few seconds, add the red chilies and the beans. Toss to mix. Add the coriander, Kashimiri chili powder, turmeric and amchoor. Mix well. Lower the heat to low and cook the beans for 10 to 15 minutes or until the beans are soft and cooked through. Add the salt and the raisins and turn off the heat.

Toss the broad beans with the nigella seeds.

Serve the apple curry hot with the crunchy green beans and the broad beans. Garnish with some micro greens.

note: *Asafetida, or Heeng in Hindi, is a pungent-smelling resin gathered from the roots of a carrot-like plant. It is used widely in Indian cooking, especially for tempering or for pickling purposes. Once cooked it lends a leek-like flavor, which even though subtle, it does enhance your dish. Asafetida acts as an umami enhancer, and my kitchen is incomplete without it.*

The spices used in the north and south of India are not that much different, but the ways of preparing a dish and also the extensive use of coconut in the south makes the flavor profiles so distinctly different. Other cultures also use coconut, but for me coconut is always reminiscent of south Indian food. I have been cooking other beans with similar ingredients but had never tried broad beans before. I was not sorry when I did. There is an irresistible crunch and flavor to this dish that leaves me wanting more.

BROAD BEAN CURRY *with* POTATO & RED PEPPER FRY

Serves 4

BROAD BEAN CURRY
1 tbsp (15 ml) oil

1 onion, finely chopped

2⅓ cups (350 g) fresh broad beans (fava beans)

½ tsp turmeric powder

1 tbsp (7 g) coriander powder

3–4 tbsp (15–20 g) desiccated coconut

1 tsp coconut sugar

1 tsp tamarind paste

Salt to taste

TEMPERING SPICES
1 tbsp (15 ml) oil

½ tsp mustard seeds

½ tsp cumin seeds

6–8 curry leaves

1–2 dried red chilies

POTATO & RED PEPPER FRY
2 tbsp (30 ml) oil

1 tsp cumin seeds

½ tsp mustard seeds

1 lb (454 g) potatoes, cut in bite-size chunks

2 red bell peppers, cut into chunks, core included

1 tbsp (7 g) coriander powder

½ tsp turmeric powder

½ tsp red chili powder

Salt to taste

For the broad bean curry, heat the oil in a pan, on high heat. Once hot, add the onion and the broad beans and cook for 8 to 10 minutes. Add the turmeric, coriander, coconut and coconut sugar. Lower the heat to low, cover the pan and simmer for 10 minutes, stirring every now and then. Add 1 tablespoon (15 ml) of water to the tamarind paste and mix to make it more fluid, and then drizzle onto the curry. Add salt and mix well.

For the tempering, heat the oil in a pan on high heat. Once hot, add the mustard and cumin seeds. Once the seeds start to sputter, in a few seconds, add the curry leaves. Then, add the red chilies. Stir and cook for just a minute and immediately transfer to the broad bean curry.

For the potato pepper fry, heat the oil in a wok on high heat. Once hot, add the cumin and mustard seeds. Once they begin to sputter, after a few seconds, add the potatoes and mix well. Lower the heat to medium-low and with the lid on, cook for 10 to 12 minutes or until the potatoes are somewhat soft. Add the peppers, coriander, turmeric and chili powder. Add the salt and stir to mix all ingredients. Cook for another 15 to 20 minutes on low heat until the potatoes and the peppers are cooked through.

Serve hot with couscous and garnish with some cilantro, pomegranate arils and some julienned beetroot.

Chickpeas are universally loved in the vegan world. I know because I am one such fan. But we rarely see black chickpeas. Which is a shame because this variety of chickpeas is fantastic for our health. Apparently just 2 to 3 tablespoons (25 to 40 g) of this magic legume can be equivalent to one portion of the daily requirement of five portions of fruit and vegetables. It has a long list of health benefits and is quite delicious in a curry and beloved in the Indian kitchen. I teamed it up with cauliflower and daikon to make it healthier and an exquisite poster child for vegan food that replaces meats so easily.

BLACK CHICKPEA CURRY *with* MADRAS CURRY CAULIFLOWER *&* DAIKON RADISH

Serves 4 to 6

BLACK CHICKPEA CURRY
¾ cup (150 g) black chickpeas (chana dal), soaked overnight

3 cups (720 ml) water

3 tbsp (45 ml) oil

1 tsp cumin seeds

1 tsp mustard seeds

1 onion, chopped fine

1 green chili, chopped

2 cloves garlic, minced

1 tomato, chopped

1 tbsp (15 ml) tomato paste

1 tsp coriander powder

½ tsp turmeric powder

½ tsp red chili powder

1 tsp chana masala

Salt to taste

MADRAS CURRY SPICE MIX
1 tbsp (5 g) coriander seeds

½ tbsp (3 g) cumin seeds

1" (2.5-cm) cinnamon stick

3 green cardamom pods

½ tbsp (6 g) fenugreek seeds

1 dried red chili

6 curry leaves

1 tbsp (7 g) turmeric powder

½ tsp black pepper

1 tsp fennel seeds

CAULIFLOWER AND DAIKON RADISH
4 tbsp (60 ml) oil, divided

3½ cups (350 g) cauliflower florets

2 medium onions, chopped

1" (2.5-cm) piece ginger, grated

¾ lb (340 g) daikon radish, cut into bite-size cubes

Salt to taste

15–18 cherry tomatoes

(continued)

BLACK CHICKPEA CURRY *with* MADRAS CURRY CAULIFLOWER & DAIKON RADISH (cont.)

Rinse the chickpeas. Combine them with the water in a pan and bring to a boil. Lower the heat to low, cover the pan and simmer for 45 minutes to an hour or until the chickpeas are cooked through. Once done, turn off the heat and set aside. Do not drain.

For the madras spice mix, in a pan on low heat, roast the coriander, cumin, cinnamon, cardamom, fenugreek, chili, curry leaves, turmeric, pepper and fennel for about a minute or until fragrant. Transfer to a spice grinder and grind to a fine powder.

For the cauliflower and radish curry, heat 1 tablespoon (15 ml) of oil in a pan on medium heat. Once hot, shallow fry the cauliflower florets for a few minutes. Once the cauliflower has slightly browned, transfer to a bowl lined with a kitchen towel. In the same pan, heat 3 tablespoons (45 ml) of oil and add the chopped onions. On medium heat, cook until the onions are translucent, 3 to 4 minutes and then add the ginger. Cook for another few minutes until the raw smell of the ginger is gone. Add the madras curry powder and stir to combine all ingredients. Add the radish and simmer and cook for 15 to 18 minutes. Add the fried cauliflower, cover the pan and cook for another 15 to 18 minutes or until the cauliflower and daikon are cooked through. Add the salt and the cherry tomatoes and turn off the heat.

For the black chickpea curry, heat the oil in a pan. Once hot, add the cumin and mustard seeds. When they start to sputter, after a few seconds, add the chopped onion, green chili and garlic and cook for 5 to 8 minutes. Add the tomato and the tomato paste and cook on medium heat for 5 minutes or until the tomato is mushy and cooked. Then add the coriander, turmeric, chili powder and chana masala and stir to mix for just a minute. Add the chickpeas with their liquid and simmer on low heat for 15 to 20 minutes or until the chickpeas are cooked through. Season with salt and turn off the heat.

Serve with basmati rice topped with the black chickpeas and the cauliflower and daikon curry on the side. Garnish with some baby spinach and cilantro and sprinkle some sunflowers seeds on top of it all.

Tofu by itself is a flavorless ingredient, but what I do love about it is that it beautifully takes on the flavors of whatever you fuse it to. Spinach with its ever-so-slightly bitter flavor goes very well with the fruity sweetness of the marinade coating the tofu. The smooth texture of the spinach is also lovely with the slight crunchiness of the sesame-coated tofu. If you ever wanted to be Popeye, this is the dish I'd go with!

SPINACH CURRY *with* DATE SYRUP SESAME TOFU & GINGER GREEN BEANS

Serves 4 to 6

DATE SYRUP TOFU MARINADE
12 oz (340 g) firm tofu
5 tbsp (75 ml) date syrup
1½ tsp (3 g) chili flakes
2 tsp (10 ml) rice vinegar
2 tsp (10 ml) sesame oil
¼ tsp sea salt
¼ cup (36 g) sesame seeds
Pinch of black pepper

SPINACH CURRY
1 lb (454 g) spinach, blanched for 2–3 minutes
2 tbsp (30 ml) olive oil
1 tsp cumin seeds
2 medium onions, chopped fine
3 cloves garlic, minced
1" (2.5-cm) piece ginger, grated
2 green chilies, slit lengthwise
2 tsp (5 g) fennel powder

2 tsp (5 g) coriander powder
½ tsp turmeric powder
1 tsp Kashmiri chili powder
½ cup (120 ml) water
3 tbsp (45 ml) date syrup
Salt to taste

GINGER GREEN BEANS
1 tbsp (15 ml) olive oil
2" (5-cm) piece ginger, cut into thin strips
1 lb (454 g) green beans, cut in half and blanched for 4–5 minutes
1½ tsp (5 g) black sesame seeds
2 tsp (10 ml) soy sauce
1 onion, sliced
Salt to taste

(continued)

SPINACH CURRY *with* DATE SYRUP SESAME TOFU & GINGER GREEN BEANS (cont.)

Drain all the liquid from the tofu. Place it on a plate lined with kitchen towels. Place more kitchen towels on top and then weigh it down with a heavy pan. Leave to rest for at least 30 minutes.

Preheat the oven to 375°F (191°C).

Make the marinade by combining the date syrup, chili flakes, vinegar, oil, salt, sesame seeds and black pepper. Stir to mix well.

Cut the drained tofu into rectangular blocks 1 inch wide and 3 inches tall (2.5 × 7.5 cm). Reserve 2 tablespoons (30 ml) of the marinade. Coat the tofu with the marinade, covering all sides. Any leftover marinade can be used to drizzle once the final dish is ready. Let the tofu marinate for at least 2 hours.

To make the spinach curry, puree the spinach in a food processor. Heat the oil in a pan on high heat. Once hot, add the cumin seeds. Once they sputter, after a few seconds, add the onions, garlic and ginger. Lower the heat to medium and cook for around 5 minutes or until the onions are translucent and browning at the edges and the raw smell of the garlic and ginger is gone. Add the green chilies and cook for another 2 minutes. Add the fennel, coriander, turmeric and chili powder. Let them cook with the onion mix for a minute and then put in the pureed spinach with the water. Stir to mix everything well. Drizzle in the date syrup and the 2 tablespoons (30 ml) of the marinade and cook for about 5 minutes. Season with salt. Turn off the heat and set aside.

Line a baking tray with parchment paper and place the marinated tofu on the tray. Bake for 15 minutes. Turn over the tofu and bake for another 15 minutes.

While the tofu bakes, make the green beans. Heat the oil in a pan on high heat. Once hot, add the ginger strips for a minute. Add the blanched green beans and toss to cook for 5 to 8 minutes on medium heat. Add the sesame seeds and cook for another few minutes. Add the soy sauce and the onion. Cook for 3 to 5 minutes, season with salt and take off the heat.

Serve hot with basmati and wild rice. Garnish with chopped spring onions.

This dish is inspired by an east Indian dish and is packed with flavors and textures of several vegetables. The silky smoothness of the eggplant and the starchy texture of the potato and pumpkin go together very well. Combined with the yummy and creamy navy beans, this is serious nourishment for your belly and soul. With every bite, you also get the surprising taste of papaya in all its grilled glory.

NAVY BEAN STEW *with* GRILLED PAPAYA

Serves 4

NAVY BEAN STEW

4 tbsp (60 g) coconut oil

1 tbsp (6 g) panch phoron spice mix

2" (5-cm) piece ginger, grated

1 potato, cut into bite-size chunks

1½ cups (210 g) peeled and chopped kabocha squash

1 eggplant, cut into large chunks

½ tbsp (4 g) turmeric powder

2 tsp (3 g) desiccated coconut

1⅔ cups (435 g) canned navy beans, rinsed and drained

3–4 tbsp (45–60 ml) water

Salt to taste

GRILLED PAPAYA

1 tsp coconut oil

2 big papayas, cut in half, seeds removed

Juice of 1 lime

For the navy bean stew, heat the oil in a pan on medium-high heat. Add the panch phoron spice mix. Once the spices sputter, after about a minute, add the ginger, lower heat to medium-low and cook for a minute. Add the potato and squash and cook for about 5 minutes until both vegetables are somewhat soft. Add the eggplant, turmeric and coconut and stir. Cook for another 10 minutes or until all the vegetables are cooked through. Add the navy beans with the water. Stir in and simmer on low heat for another 10 minutes. Season with salt and turn off the heat.

While the curry is cooking, heat a grill pan and add the coconut oil. Drizzle the papayas with lime juice and place face down and grill for 4 to 5 minutes or until slightly charred. Serve by scooping the navy bean stew into the papaya halves. Garnish with cilantro and chia seeds and a dash of lime.

Nice & Slow
PLANT-BASED DELIGHTS

Indian food is all about an overload of masalas (spices) and a generous helping of love thrown in to make it the delicious and popular food that it is. For my mother, weekday cooking with all the fresh produce was mostly with just three masalas: coriander, chili and turmeric powder. To this day, almost all my cooking is based on these three spices. I rarely go without one or all three. On the weekends however, we got treats of the rich curry kind. Hours spent in the kitchen, grinding fresh masala blends and roasting them lovingly with all sorts of vegetables in season.

This section doesn't require you to perhaps spend hours in the kitchen like my mom did, but it will require relaxed time to cook at leisure. And while you pour yourself a glass of wine, you will discover how intensely cathartic and meditative it might be as you prepare all your masalas, mindfully cook all your vegetables and smell the fresh aromas of the happy unions float through the house.

This dish comes from the western region of India, called Rajasthan. Eaten in the winter months when the turmeric root is in season, this curry has immense healing powers and benefits for your health. Not many people, even in India, know of this beautiful sunset-colored curry. It's known as the poor man's saffron because of its appealing sunny disposition; this is, however, a curry fit for kings. The original version uses a massive amount of ghee (clarified butter), but can easily be replaced with generous amounts of plant-based oil.

RAW TURMERIC & CAULIFLOWER CURRY

Serves 6

10 tbsp (150 ml) oil, divided

2 cups (200 g) cauliflower florets

¼ tsp asafetida

¼ tsp mustard seeds

1 tsp cumin seeds

½ lb (225 g) raw turmeric root, peeled and grated

1 tbsp (5 g) coriander powder

1 tsp chili powder

½ tsp garam masala

1 cup (240 ml) coconut milk

1 large onion, pureed

1" (2.5-cm) piece ginger, grated

4 cloves garlic, minced

1 green chili, chopped

1 large fresh tomato, pureed

3 tbsp (45 ml) tomato paste

Salt to taste

Heat 2 tablespoons (30 ml) of oil in a wide pan on medium heat. Shallow fry the cauliflower florets for a few minutes or until they are soft. Drain and transfer to a bowl lined with kitchen towels.

In the same pan, heat 2 more tablespoons (30 ml) of oil on high heat. Once hot, add the asafetida, mustard and cumin seeds. Once they start to sputter, after a few seconds, lower heat to medium and add the grated turmeric and shallow fry for 4 to 5 minutes, stirring regularly. The turmeric should turn golden yellow. Once done, transfer to a separate dish and set aside.

In a bowl, add the coriander powder, chili powder and garam masala to the coconut milk. Mix well and set aside.

In the same pan where the turmeric was fried, heat the rest of the oil on high heat. Once hot, add the onion, ginger, garlic and green chili. Cook for 5 to 6 minutes, stirring often. Lower heat to medium and add the pureed tomato and the tomato paste and stir to combine. Cook until the oil leaves the sides of the pan and the tomato is cooked, around 10 minutes. Add the coconut milk mix and stir to combine. Cover the pan and simmer on low heat for 15 to 18 minutes. Stir every now and then. Halfway through, add the fried cauliflower. Cover the pan again and cook for the remainder of the time. Season with salt and turn off the heat.

Garnish the dish with some green peas and cilantro. Serve with hot rotis.

Oddly enough, the oven is never really used in India for cooking savory dishes, but baking is a wonderful option for an easier, healthier recipe and the flavor still remains fantastic. Raita is eaten in India to combat spicy dishes and to cool the palate. In this recipe it serves the same purpose with the added crunchiness of the pomegranate arils. A satisfying, filling meal, this meal shows off the power of vegetable and legume combinations.

SPICY ADZUKI BEAN-STUFFED EGGPLANT BOATS with POMEGRANATE COCONUT RAITA

Serves 4

½ cup (108 g) adzuki beans, soaked overnight

2 cups (480 ml) water

2 small eggplants (about 8 oz [200 g] each), halved

Salt to taste

1 tbsp (15 ml) oil, divided

FILLING

2 tbsp (30 ml) oil

2 shallots, chopped

1 clove garlic, minced

1 green chili, chopped fine

1 tsp nigella seeds (kalonji)

1 medium tomato, chopped

½ cup (120 ml) tomato puree

½ tsp cumin powder

1 tsp Kashmiri chili powder

1 tsp lime juice

1 cup (186 g) cooked basmati rice

Salt to taste

COCONUT POMEGRANATE RAITA

1 cup (240 ml) coconut yogurt

½ cup (87 g) pomegranate arils

1 tsp cumin powder

¼ tsp Kashmiri chili powder

½ tsp black salt

8–10 mint leaves, chopped

Preheat the oven to 400°F (205°C).

Combine the beans with the water in a pan and bring to a boil on high heat. Then lower the heat and simmer with the lid on for 30 to 35 minutes or until the beans are cooked through. They should be slightly firm, holding their shape. Cut the eggplants lengthwise in half and scoop out the flesh, reserving it for the filling. Sprinkle the scooped-out flesh and the eggplant skins generously with salt and set the flesh aside.

Rub half of the oil onto the skin of the eggplants and heat the other half over medium-high heat in a grill pan. Place the eggplants cut side down in the pan. Roast each side for 3 to 4 minutes on medium heat or until the eggplant is slightly charred. Once done place each half, cut side up, on its own piece of foil on a baking tray and let cool.

To prepare the filling, heat the oil in a pan and add the shallots, garlic and green chili. Cook on medium heat until the shallots just start to brown, 1 to 2 minutes. Add the nigella seeds and the eggplant flesh and cook until the eggplant is soft and mushy, 4 to 5 minutes. Add the chopped tomato and the tomato puree with the cumin, chili powder and lime juice and mix well, cooking for 3 to 4 minutes. Add the cooked adzuki beans and rice and season with salt. Mix well.

Scoop the filling into the eggplant boats and seal with foil. Bake for 15 to 20 minutes or until the eggplant is soft and cooked through.

While the eggplants are baking, make the raita by combining the yogurt, pomegranate, cumin, chili powder, salt and mint. Mix well and keep aside.

Serve the eggplants hot with a dollop of the raita on top and garnished with chopped cilantro and pomegranate arils.

Dal makhani is one of the most loved dals and almost always on the menu at any restaurant serving Indian food. It is creamy and extremely filling. You could eat this dal all by itself as a meal or eat it with a roti or naan like the Indians do. Either way or fashion, it is a gorgeously creamy, yummy dal. I have used coconut oil in place of the ghee or butter, which didn't change its flavor much but sure made it healthier!

NO BUTTER DAL MAKHANI

Serves 4

¾ cup (150 g) whole black gram beans (whole urad dal)

¼ cup (50 g) red kidney beans

4 cups (960 ml) + ¼ cup (60 ml) water, divided

1 tsp salt

4 tbsp (60 g) coconut oil

1 tbsp (6 g) cumin seeds

Pinch of cinnamon

1 black cardamom pod

2–3 whole cloves

2 green cardamom pods

1 small bay leaf

3 small onions, chopped

1" (2.5-cm) piece ginger, crushed

6–8 cloves garlic, crushed

1–2 green chilies, chopped

3 medium tomatoes, pureed

½ tsp turmeric powder

2 tsp (5 g) Kashmiri chili powder (reduce to half if using regular chili powder)

3 tbsp (45 ml) tomato paste

Salt to taste

1 tbsp (2 g) dried fenugreek leaves (kasturi methi)

Soak the beans overnight or for at least 7 to 8 hours.

Rinse the beans, and place them both in a pressure cooker with 4 cups (960 ml) water. Add the salt and close the lid of the pressure cooker. Cook on high heat and wait until it gives 8 to 10 whistles. Lower the heat to low and cook for another 30 minutes.

In a nonstick deep pan, heat the coconut oil on medium heat and add the cumin seeds, cinnamon, black cardamom, cloves, green cardamoms and bay leaf. Let steep for around 2 minutes, stirring occasionally, until the coconut oil is fragrant with the spices.

Add the chopped onions and sauté until golden brown in color. Add the ginger and garlic and cook until the raw smell of the ginger and garlic are gone, around 3 to 4 minutes. Add the chopped green chilies and the pureed fresh tomatoes and cook this mixture until the oil releases from the sides of the pan or for 15 to 20 minutes on medium-low heat. Halfway through this, add the turmeric, Kashmiri chili powder and the tomato paste.

Once the tomato mixture is cooked, add the cooked beans. Add the ¼ cup (60 ml) water, or more if you want the dal thinner, and salt and mix well. On low heat, cook for at least 30 minutes. I sometimes let it simmer away for 45 minutes.

Turn off the heat, crush the fenugreek leaves on top of the dal, stir and garnish with cilantro leaves and a swirl of coconut milk and add some red onion slices. Serve fresh with roti or naan.

Bharta, fire-roasted eggplant, is a household favorite in India. In this version I have combined the eggplants with the chana dal. The chana dal makes for a beautifully textured dal and the roasted eggplant adds that extra smoky flavor.

FIRE-ROASTED EGGPLANT TWO-LENTIL DAL

Serves 4

TWO-LENTIL DAL

½ cup (100 g) split chickpeas (chana dal), soaked for 2 hours

¼ cup (54 g) split and dehusked mung beans (split and dehusked moong dal), soaked for 2 hours

2½ cups (600 ml) water

FIRE-ROASTED EGGPLANTS

2 small eggplants (200 g each)

3 tbsp + 1 tsp (50 ml) oil, divided

1 heaped tsp cumin seeds

2 small red onions, chopped fine

3–4 cloves garlic, minced

1"(2.5-cm) piece ginger, shredded

2 small tomatoes, chopped

½ tsp turmeric powder

½ tsp red chili powder

Salt to taste

FIRE-ROASTED EGGPLANT TEMPERING

2 tbsp + ½ tsp (35 ml) oil, divided

1 small eggplant (200 g)

1 small onion, sliced fine

1 red chili, chopped

3 cloves garlic, sliced

1 tomato, sliced

½ tsp red chili powder

Salt to taste

Rinse the split chickpeas and beans under cold water. Combine them in a pan with the water and bring to a boil over high heat. Once it comes to a boil, lower the heat to low. Remove any foam with a spoon. Put the lid on and let simmer, covered, for around 25 minutes or until the chickpeas and the beans are tender and cooked through. Do not drain.

Wash the eggplants and dry them before rubbing them with 1 teaspoon of oil. Turn on two gas burners and place an eggplant on each open fire. Char the eggplants for 8 to 10 minutes, turning them with a pair of tongs to get all sides equally roasted. Turn off the burners and set the eggplants aside on a plate to cool down. Once cool, remove the charred skin. It will come off with ease. Don't worry about any small pieces of charred skin that you cannot remove. Mash the eggplants coarsely with a fork or simply with your fingers.

In a pan, heat the rest of the oil on high heat. Once hot, add the cumin seeds. Once they start to sputter, after a few seconds, add the chopped onions, garlic and ginger. Cook on medium heat until the onions start to brown and the raw smell of the ginger and garlic is gone, around 3 to 4 minutes. Add the tomatoes, turmeric and chili powder and cook until oil starts to release, around 10 minutes. The tomatoes will be mushy by now. Add the mashed eggplant and mix well. Add salt and cook on high heat for a few minutes and then lower the heat and cook for another 5 to 8 minutes, stirring occasionally.

Add the cooked peas and beans with their liquid to the eggplant curry mixture. Combine to mix well and simmer on low heat while you prepare the tempering.

For the tempering, rub ½ teaspoon of oil on the surface of the eggplant and turn a gas burner on high. Char this eggplant very slightly, 3 to 4 minutes on the open fire. Set aside to cool, and then cut the eggplant into large cubes. Heat the rest of the oil in a pan. Once hot, add the onion, red chili and garlic, stirring often. Cook on high heat, stirring often, until the onion begins to brown, around 5 minutes. Add the eggplant cubes and cook on medium-high heat until the eggplant is soft but has not fallen apart, 8 to 10 minutes. Add the tomato, red chili powder and the salt, cooking for just 2 to 3 minutes so that the tomato doesn't completely fall apart. Add the tempering to the top of the eggplant dal and serve hot with garlic cilantro naan.

As children, if we were good, we were treated to a special dish called *chole* (chickpea masala). Mouthwatering and spicy, we ate it with glee, licking our fingers after we had scooped every bite with our fresh Indian bread. This version is my take on that dish with the addition of vegetables and a huge coconut flavor. It makes it creamier rather than tangier, making it unlike the original but just as yummy.

COCONUT CHICKPEA CURRY *with* BROCCOLI & BELL PEPPER

Serves 4

ROASTED SPICE MIX

5 tbsp (27 g) desiccated coconut

1 tsp fennel seeds

1 tsp cumin seeds

½" (13-mm) cinnamon stick

2 green cardamom pods

3 whole cloves

CHICKPEA CURRY

1 cup (200 g) dry chickpeas (chana dal), soaked for 8–10 hours (or 3 cups [720 g] canned chickpeas)

¼ cup (50 g) red kidney beans, soaked for 8–10 hours (or ½ cup [130 g] canned kidney beans)

4 cups (960 ml) + ¾ cup (180 ml) water, divided

3 tbsp (45 g) coconut oil

¼ tsp mustard seeds

¾ tsp cumin seeds

1" (2.5-cm) piece ginger, grated

3 cloves garlic, minced

1–2 green chilies, chopped

2 small onions, chopped

½ tsp turmeric powder

1 tsp Kashmiri chili powder

1 tsp coriander powder

2 tbsp (30 ml) tomato ketchup

1½ cups (135 g) broccoli florets

1 red bell pepper, cut into chunks

1 cup (240 ml) coconut milk

For the spice mix, dry roast the desiccated coconut, fennel, cumin, cinnamon, cardamom and cloves until golden brown in a pan over medium-high heat. Coriander seeds always roast the fastest, so make sure you stir often. Once ready, grind to a smooth powder with a mortar and pestle or spice grinder.

Rinse the chickpeas and kidney beans under cold water 2 to 3 times. In a pot, combine the chickpeas with 4 cups (960 ml) water and bring to a boil over high heat. Once the chickpeas come to a boil, lower the heat to low. Remove any foam with a spoon. Let simmer, covered, for 30 to 35 minutes. In a separate pot, cover the kidney beans with water, bring to a boil, and then lower the heat to low. Cook for 50 to 60 minutes. When cooked, drain and set aside. Skip this step if using canned beans. Heat the oil in a pan over medium-high heat. Once hot, add the mustard and cumin seeds. Once they begin to sputter, after a few seconds, lower heat to medium and add the ginger, garlic and chopped chilies. Cook until the raw smell of the ginger and garlic is gone, around 2 to 3 minutes. Add the onions and cook until the onions begin to turn a little brown, 4 to 5 minutes. Add the turmeric, Kashmiri chili powder and the coriander and stir to mix. Add the roasted spice mix, tomato ketchup and ¼ cup (60 ml) of water and stir again to mix well. Cook for 5 to 6 minutes.

Add the broccoli and the pepper to this spice mixture. Stir to mix the spices with the vegetables. Lower the heat to low and let the vegetables soak in the spices for 4 to 5 minutes. Raise the heat to medium-high again and cook for 5 to 8 minutes. Add the chickpeas and the red kidney beans and stir to combine it with all the spices and the vegetables. Add the coconut milk and ½ cup (120 ml) of water, cover the pan and let simmer for 15 to 18 minutes on low heat or until the vegetables are soft but not falling apart.

Serve with chopped cilantro sprinkled on top and scoop with bhaturas.

Even though we ate stuffed vegetables at times, it was definitely not the norm. I still don't think of doing it often enough in my daily meals. And especially not with potatoes. There is a huge variety in cooking methods for potatoes in India, with some stuffed versions, but none of them involve stuffing them in this way. Potatoes make a perfect vessel for stuffing because they take on other flavors so wonderfully. This version is stuffed with tangy legumes, offset with a creamy cashew sauce and is again a wonderful example of how satisfying a vegan meal can be.

BAKED SWEET POTATO STUFFED
with CHANA MASALA LENTILS & CASHEW CREAM

Serves 2–3

2 medium sweet potatoes, scrubbed clean

FILLING
2 tbsp (30 ml) oil

1 red onion, chopped

1 tsp oregano

1 red chili, chopped

3 cloves garlic, minced

3 tbsp (45 ml) tomato paste

1 tsp chana masala

5–6 sun-dried tomatoes, cut into strips

8–10 black olives

1 cup (240 g) canned brown lentils (whole masoor dal)

½ cup (130 g) canned red kidney beans

Salt and pepper to taste

CASHEW CREAM
½ cup (65 g) unsalted cashews, soaked for 2 hours

1 clove garlic

½ cup (120 ml) water

Preheat the oven to 400°F (205°C). Line a baking tray with foil.

Poke the potatoes with a fork and set them on the baking tray. Bake for 40 to 45 minutes or until completely cooked through. A knife should slide through easily.

For the filling, heat the oil in a pan on high heat. Once hot, add the onion and cook until the onion begins to brown a little, 2 to 3 minutes. Lower the heat to medium and add the oregano, chili and garlic. Cook until the raw smell of the garlic is gone, 2 to 3 minutes. Add the tomato paste and mix well. Add the chana masala, sun-dried tomatoes and black olives. Cook for another few minutes. Add the lentils and the kidney beans and let the filling simmer on low heat for a few minutes. Add the salt and pepper.

Drain the soaked cashews and add them to a food processor with the garlic clove and water and blitz until a very smooth paste. This will take 5 to 7 minutes on high speed. Once done, transfer to a bowl and set aside.

Cut open the sweet potatoes, add a scoop of the lentil-bean filling and top with some chopped onion, tomatoes and parsley. Drizzle with the cashew cream and serve hot.

At Diwali time, Mom always made a potato and tomato curry. It was a tradition that we looked forward to. It was a very simple dish served with homemade Indian bread called pooris. I have deconstructed this beloved dish into smashed potatoes that are baked and laid on a bed on top of the tomato curry and topped with spinach pesto. One word: divine.

TOMATO & SMASHED POTATO CURRY *with* SPINACH PESTO

Serves 4

SMASHED POTATOES
2¼ lbs (1 kg) small potatoes
1½ tsp (7 ml) olive oil
2 tsp (4 g) carom seeds
Salt and pepper to taste

SPINACH PESTO
2 cups (60 g) spinach, packed
¼ cup (30 g) unsalted pistachios
2 cloves garlic
1 tsp lemon juice
½ cup (120 ml) olive oil
Salt and pepper to taste

TOMATO CURRY
1 tbsp (15 ml) olive oil
1 tsp carom seeds
1 onion, sliced
3–4 cloves garlic, crushed
1" (2.5-cm) piece ginger, crushed
4 medium tomatoes, sliced
Salt and pepper to taste

Preheat the oven to 400°F (205°C).

Line a baking tray with parchment paper or brush your baking tray with oil.

Cook the potatoes in water for 20 to 25 minutes or until a knife can pierce them easily. Drain and allow the potatoes to cool.

Combine the olive oil, carom seeds, salt and pepper in a bowl.

When the potatoes are cool, transfer them to the baking tray and press down on each one with a potato masher or with the back of a fork to smash them. Brush them with the olive oil and carom seeds mixture and bake for 20 to 25 minutes.

Make the pesto by blitzing the spinach, pistachios, garlic, lemon juice, oil, salt and pepper together in a food processor to form a smooth paste. Transfer to a bowl.

For the tomato curry, heat the oil in a pan on high heat. Once hot, add the carom seeds. Cook for about a minute, lower heat to medium and then add the onion, garlic and ginger. Cook until the onion starts to brown and the raw smell of the garlic and ginger is gone, 3 to 4 minutes. Add the sliced tomatoes and simmer for 8 to 10 minutes or until the tomatoes are mushy. Add salt and pepper and turn off the heat.

To serve, pour the tomato curry onto a serving platter. Place the smashed potatoes on top. Add generous dollops of pesto and garnish with extra pistachios and baby spinach leaves.

Cauliflower was my favorite winter vegetable, and my mother made some pretty good versions of it. Cauliflower, unlike most veggies, takes on masalas very well. It can taste distinctly different with different spice mixes and therefore works very well in curries. Steeping it in the peanut coconut spices makes yet another new, super delicious way to eat it for me, and I hope for you too.

PEANUT, CAULIFLOWER & POTATO CURRY

Serves 4

PEANUT COCONUT PASTE
½ cup (65 g) roasted peanuts
4–5 cloves garlic
1½ tbsp (7 g) toasted desiccated coconut

CAULIFLOWER AND POTATO CURRY
6 tbsp (90 ml) olive oil
4–5 curry leaves
1 tsp mustard seeds
1 tsp cumin seeds
⅛ tsp asafetida
⅛ tsp fenugreek seeds
½ tsp nigella seeds (kalonji)
1 tsp Kashmiri chili powder
1 tsp turmeric powder
1½ tsp (3 g) coriander powder
3 onions, chopped
1 tbsp (14 g) brown sugar
Salt to taste
3–4 medium potatoes, cut into cubes
4 cups (400 g) cauliflower florets
½ cup (120 ml) water
1 tbsp (15 ml) tamarind paste
1 tbsp (13 g) coconut sugar
Pepper to taste

Grind together the peanuts, garlic and coconut in a spice grinder to a fine paste. Set aside.

For the curry, heat the oil in a wok or a deep pan, on high heat. Once hot, add the curry leaves. Once they start to change color and sputter, in a few seconds, add the mustard, cumin, asafetida, fenugreek and nigella seeds. Once the spices start to sputter, after another few seconds, reduce the heat to medium and add the chili powder, turmeric and coriander. Cook while stirring for a few minutes and then add the onions, brown sugar and some salt. Cook until the onions are browning, 4 to 5 minutes. Add the peanut-coconut paste and continue to cook for another 4 to 5 minutes.

Add the potatoes and simmer, covered, on low heat for about 10 minutes. Add the cauliflower florets, water, tamarind paste, coconut sugar, salt and pepper. Stir to combine, cover and simmer for 30 to 40 minutes or until the cauliflower and the potatoes are cooked through. Garnish with cilantro, toasted coconut flakes and roasted peanuts.

Serve hot with cumin rice.

Lentils always spell comfort for me, whether in an elaborate curry, dal or in a salad. It's not uncommon to eat sprouted lentils as a salad in India, and it is one of the most beneficial things you can eat. I like cooking my sprouts with some onions for a minute or two with just pepper and salt. In this recipe I have used the African spice ras el hanout, which gives a warm coziness to this salad. I prepare this dish by assembling it hours before. When you are actually ready to eat, the beet color and flavor will have permeated through to the coconut yogurt. Delicious to eat and beautiful to look at.

SPROUTED MOTH BEANS *with* ROASTED BEETS & BEET-INFUSED COCONUT YOGURT

Serves 4

4 medium beetroots

MOTH BEANS
1 tsp oil
1 tsp cumin seeds
1 medium red onion, chopped
1 tsp ras el hanout
1 cup (200 g) sprouted moth beans

COCONUT YOGURT
1 cup (240 ml) coconut yogurt
Salt and pepper

Preheat the oven to 400°F (205°C). Prepare a baking tray lined with parchment paper.

Wash the beetroots well and cover each one loosely and separately in foil. Place them on the baking tray. Bake for 50 to 60 minutes or until a knife enters the flesh easily. Halfway through, check to see if the beets are getting dry. If dry, add a little water in the foil pouch. Allow the beets to cool and then peel and quarter them.

While the beetroots are roasting, prepare the moth beans. Heat the oil in a pan on high heat. Add the cumin seeds. Once they start to sputter, after a few seconds, lower the heat to medium and add the red onion and cook until the onion begins to brown, 3 to 4 minutes. Add the ras el hanout and stir to mix. Cook for 30 seconds. Add the moth beans and cook for no more than 2 to 3 minutes. Turn off the heat.

In a small bowl, mix together the coconut yogurt, salt and pepper.

To serve, spread a layer of the coconut yogurt on a platter. Top with the sprouted moth beans and the beet chunks and finish with micro greens, red onion and roasted cashews.

note: *I always have sprouted beans at my house, and they are fairly easy to do. You don't need any equipment except for a fine muslin cloth.*

Soak the beans overnight. In the morning, rinse a few times under cold water and then transfer to a muslin cloth large enough to hold the beans. Place the beans held by the muslin cloth in a large bowl, fold the muslin over the top and leave to rest.

The next morning repeat the process of rinsing the beans. In 2 days you should have your sprouted beans.

This dish is usually made with baby eggplants that are stuffed with the exotic peanut spice mix. Baby eggplants are hard to find in Holland, so I've cooked the eggplants with the filling instead of stuffing them with it. The result is unbelievably tasty and wholesome, silky and mouth watering.

PEANUT & EGGPLANT CURRY

Serves 4 to 6

ROASTED SPICE MIX

½ cup (65 g) peanuts

2 tbsp (18 g) sesame seeds

2 tsp (6 g) poppy seeds

1 tbsp (5 g) coriander seeds

1 tsp cumin seeds

2 tbsp (10 g) desiccated coconut

CURRY

6–7 tbsp (90–105 ml) oil

3 medium onions, finely chopped

2"(5-cm) piece ginger, grated

5–6 cloves garlic, minced

½ tsp turmeric powder

2 tsp (5 g) Kashmiri chili powder

2 tbsp (26 g) coconut sugar

2 tbsp (30 ml) tamari soy sauce

2 big eggplants, cut into big chunks

For the spice mix, roast the peanuts, sesame seeds, poppy seeds, coriander, cumin and coconut in a pan for a minute on medium heat or until the spices are fragrant and slightly brown. Transfer to a spice grinder and grind to a fine powder.

For the curry, heat the oil in a pan on high heat. Once hot, add the chopped onions. Cook the onions while stirring regularly for 8 to 10 minutes or until they are golden brown. Lower the heat to medium, add the ginger and garlic and cook for an additional few minutes until the raw smell of the spices is gone. Now add the roasted spice mix and stir well to combine. Cook for 4 to 5 minutes and then add the turmeric, chili powder and coconut sugar and cook for 4 to 5 minutes more. Add the soy sauce and stir for just a minute before adding the eggplants. Cover and simmer on low heat for 35 to 40 minutes or until the eggplants are soft and cooked through. Garnish with cilantro.

Serve hot with garlic naan.

note: *Roasting spices is an everyday thing in India and in my kitchen. I only dry roast whole spices and not ones that are already ground. The roasting process releases the oils from the whole spices and makes not only your kitchen but also your dish fragrant. Over-roasting the spices will make their taste bitter, so pay attention. Once done, grind to a fine powder.*

This dish is based on my all-time favorite recipe called rajma. I loved it so much that growing up my mother made it for me every weekend, without fail. Mom used to always make a little extra so that I could snack on it the enitre day. There are two camps in the rajma curry area, one that uses red kidney beans and the other that uses borlotti beans. I belong to the latter. I have changed this famous darling of almost every Indian dish with ingredients not used in the original recipe—it now closely resembles a chili.

RAJMA CHILI CURRY

Serves 4 to 6

1½ cups (300 g) borlotti beans, soaked overnight

4 cups (960 ml) water

4 tbsp (60 ml) oil

2 medium onions, chopped

6 cloves garlic, crushed

3 green chilies (add more or less according to taste)

2 tbsp (17 g) cumin powder

½ tbsp (4 g) Kashmiri chili powder

2 tsp (5 g) paprika powder (smoked or plain)

1 tsp dried oregano

8–10 fresh basil leaves, chopped

¼ tsp cayenne pepper

1 tbsp (6 g) Italian seasoning

½ tsp coriander powder

2 bell peppers (any color), chopped

1⅔ cups (400 g) canned tomatoes

2 tbsp (30 ml) tomato paste

1 cup (155 g) fresh (or frozen) corn kernels

Salt to taste

Rinse the beans. If using a pressure cooker, combine the beans with the water and after giving them 2 to 3 whistles, simmer on low heat for 20 minutes. If not using a pressure cooker, combine the beans with the same amount of water in a pan and bring to a boil. Simmer, covered, for 30 to 40 minutes or until the beans are soft and cooked. Do not drain.

In a deep pan, heat the oil on high heat. Once hot, add the onions and cook until the onions are browning slightly at the edges, 4 to 6 minutes. Add the garlic and green chilies and cook for 2 minutes. Lower the heat to medium and add the cumin, Kashmiri chili powder, paprika, dried oregano, basil leaves, cayenne pepper, Italian seasoning and coriander. Cook for just 2 minutes, until the spices are fragrant, stirring to combine all the ingredients. Add the bell peppers and simmer for around 10 minutes on low heat until the bell peppers are somewhat soft. Add the canned tomatoes and tomato paste and stir to combine. Cook for another 10 minutes, stirring every now and then. Add the cooked beans and the corn kernels and simmer for another 10 to 12 minutes on low heat. Add the salt and turn off the heat. Garnish with cilantro.

Serve with basmati rice and some salad.

I am obsessed with using greens with curries the past couple of years. It is a great way to hide greens if you have a picky eater at home. Greens also add a lot of texture to a curry. Black-eyed peas are prepared almost always with tomatoes and a ton of spices in India. Here I have tried to mix the Indian with the West by using sage and tofu as flavors. This dish is surprising for my Indian palate because of how mild and surprisingly fresh it is.

LOBIA CURRY *with* ENDIVE & TOFU

Serves 4 to 6

1½ cups (380 g) firm tofu

4 tbsp (60 ml) olive oil

2 medium onions

1 green chili, chopped

1 tsp fennel seeds

6 cloves garlic, crushed

1 tbsp (4 g) chopped fresh sage

Zest of 1 lemon

1 cup (145 g) black-eyed peas (lobia), soaked overnight

3 cups (720 ml) water

4 oz (112 g) endive, roughly torn

1 tsp lemon juice

½ cup (70 g) green olives

1 tsp garam masala

Salt and pepper to taste

Drain the tofu by putting it on a plate lined with a kitchen towel. Cover the tofu with some more kitchen towels, place a heavy weight on top and let sit for at least 30 minutes. Once drained, cut it into rectangular pieces. Set aside.

In a large, deep pan, heat the oil on medium heat. Once hot, add the onions and green chili and cook until the onions are translucent and browning slightly at the edges, around 10 minutes. Add the fennel seeds and let them cook for about a minute or until fragrant. Reduce the heat to low, add the garlic and stir and cook for around 5 minutes. Add the sage and the lemon zest and cook for about a minute. Add the peas with the water and simmer for 70 to 80 minutes or until the peas are cooked through.

Once the peas are cooked, add the endive and stir until wilted, around 5 minutes. Add the lemon juice and the tofu. Cook for 5 minutes. At the very end, add the green olives and sprinkle the garam masala. Stir and season with salt and pepper.

Serve hot with noodles.

Mom always said that the taste of a dish, that magic flavor, lies in the hands of the person cooking the dish. It is how much you love to do something that will make the difference. I really believe that. Ratatouille is a perfect example of a dish that has almost everything thrown in. By itself, it's extremely simple except for the magic in the hands of the person creating it. I have tried to make this a spicier, more Indian version with some spicy koftas. In my case, the magic lies in the collaboration of the koftas with the ratatouille.

RATATOUILLE CURRY *with* ZUCCHINI TOFU KOFTAS

Serves 4

RATATOUILLE

2 tbsp (30 ml) olive oil

1 tsp cumin seeds

2 bell peppers, red and yellow, cut into small pieces

2 cups (230 g) zucchini, sliced in strips

3 medium onions, chopped

1 tbsp (7 g) paprika powder

½ tsp Kashmiri chili powder

2 tsp (2 g) dried thyme

4 medium tomatoes

2 cups (480 g) canned tomatoes

2 tsp (5 g) garlic powder

1 tsp dried oregano

2 tbsp (30 ml) tomato ketchup

Salt and pepper to taste

KOFTAS

2 cups (260 g) grated zucchini

1 cup (240 g) grated tofu

1 medium onion, chopped fine

3 tbsp (17 g) chickpea flour (besan)

2 tbsp (14 g) bread crumbs

1 tsp turmeric powder

2–3 green chilies, chopped

1" (2.5-cm) piece ginger, grated

3–4 cloves garlic, minced

Salt to taste

Oil for deep-frying

For the ratatouille, heat the oil in a pan on high heat. Once hot, add the cumin seeds. Once they sputter, after a few seconds, add the bell peppers and cook until the peppers are slightly charred, 5 minutes. Add the zucchini and cook for about 5 minutes. Add the onions and cook until the onions are translucent, 3 to 4 minutes. Add the paprika, chili powder and thyme. Cook for just 2 minutes, then add the tomatoes and the canned tomatoes and stir to mix well. Lower the heat to medium and simmer for 10 minutes. At 5 minutes, add the garlic powder and oregano. Continue to stir and add the tomato ketchup. Simmer for another 5 minutes. Season with salt and pepper.

For the koftas, peel the zucchini and grate it. Because zucchinis hold a lot of water, squeeze out as much liquid as you can. Transfer to a bowl and add the tofu, onion, flour, bread crumbs, turmeric, chilies, ginger, garlic and salt. Mix well with your fingers. Add a little oil to your palms and divide the mixture into somewhat equal portions. Form balls out of the mixture. You should be able to form 12 to 15 balls.

Heat enough oil for deep-frying in a wok. Once it is hot, reduce the heat to medium and add 3 or 4 balls at a time. Stirring occasionally, deep-fry the koftas until golden brown. Drain off the excess oil using a slotted spoon and place on a plate lined with a kitchen towel. Repeat until all your koftas are ready. Set aside.

Add the kofta balls to the ratatouille. Season with chopped cilantro and roasted cashews.

I looked high and low for fenugreek leaves in Holland. It's a delicious, slightly bitter green we use a lot in India in curries and also in our flatbreads. I finally found them at a site only for it to be out of stock for weeks on end. On my weekly visit to the farmers' market, I found one vendor selling bagfuls of a certain leafy green. On asking what it was, I was disappointed to find that it was a green called *postelein*. I nearly walked away but then decided to replace the fenugreek leaves with this new green. In the end, I am glad I never found the fenugreek leaves because *postelein*, or purslane in English, is a lovely green with a mild citric flavor. It also combined very well with the intense masala chickpeas cooked slowly with spices and tea.

MASALA CHICKPEA CURRY *with* PURSLANE

Serves 4

ROASTED SPICE MIX
1½ tbsp (7 g) coriander seeds

3–4 whole cloves

1"(2.5-cm) cinnamon stick

1 black cardamom pod

½ tsp peppercorns

1 tsp cumin seeds

CHICKPEA CURRY
1 cup (200 g) chickpeas, soaked overnight

4 cups (960 ml) water

1"(2.5-cm) cinnamon stick

1 black cardamom pod

Pinch of baking soda

1 black tea bag

4 tbsp (60 ml) oil

2 medium onions, chopped

1"(2.5-cm) piece ginger, grated

4 cloves garlic, minced

2–3 green chilies, sliced lengthwise

1 tbsp (15 ml) tomato paste

1⅔ cups (400 g) canned tomatoes

Salt to taste

1 tbsp (7 g) paprika powder

¼ tsp cayenne pepper

½ tsp Kashmiri chili powder

½ tsp amchoor powder

4 oz (112 g) purslane

(continued)

MASALA CHICKPEA CURRY *with* PURSLANE (cont.)

For the spice mix, dry roast the coriander, cloves, cinnamon, cardamom, peppercorns and cumin in a pan for just a minute until they are nice and fragrant and slightly brown. Transfer to a spice grinder and grind to a fine powder.

Rinse the chickpeas a few times and then transfer to a pot and combine with the water, cinnamon, black cardamom, baking soda and a tea bag. Bring to a boil, lower the heat to low and simmer for 40 to 45 minutes or until the chickpeas are soft but not mushy and cooked through. Reserve 1 cup (240 ml) of liquid from the cooked chickpeas to use later and discard the tea bag and the rest of the cooking liquid.

While the chickpeas are cooking, prepare the curry. In a pan, heat the oil on high heat. Once hot, add the onions, ginger, garlic and green chilies. Cook for around 10 minutes on medium heat, or until the raw smell of the ginger and garlic is gone. Add the tomato paste and canned tomatoes and stir to mix well with the onion mixture. Cook while stirring for 5 to 6 minutes. Once the tomatoes are well incorporated, season with salt and add the roasted spices, paprika powder, cayenne pepper and the Kashmiri chili powder. Mix well and cook for a minute or two.

Lower the heat to low and add the chickpeas and the reserved chickpea stock, plus the amchoor powder. Simmer with the lid on for 15 to 20 minutes.

At the very end, add the purslane leaves and cook until they are a little wilted, 3 to 4 minutes. Garnish with some fresh purslane leaves, cherry tomatoes and roasted almonds. Serve hot with paranthas.

No one would dream of making naan at home in India. It was something to order when eating out. I think we always assumed that it needed a *tandoor* oven. The thing is, it is really easy to make. And they always come out so good. Labor intensive yes, but so worth it! These naans also serve as great tacos with my Indianized version of falafels with green peas and a spicy mouthwatering avocado chutney.

NAAN TACOS *with* GREEN PEA AMARANTH FALAFELS & SPICY AVOCADO CHUTNEY

Serves 4 to 6

GARLIC OIL
1 clove garlic, minced
1 tsp oil

GARLIC NAAN
1 tsp sugar
½ cup + 1 tbsp (135 ml) warm water
2 tsp (8 g) dried active yeast
3 cups (375 g) all-purpose flour
½ tsp salt
1 tbsp (15 ml) oil

AVOCADO CHUTNEY
1 avocado
1 cup (16 g) packed cilantro
¼ cup (6 g) packed mint
1 tbsp (15 ml) coconut yogurt
1 green chili
Juice of ½ lemon
Salt and pepper to taste

GARLIC TURMERIC TAHINI SAUCE
½ cup (120 ml) tahini
2 tbsp (30 ml) water
1 clove garlic, minced
½ tsp turmeric powder
1 tsp lemon juice
Salt to taste

FALAFEL
2½ cups (400 g) canned chickpeas, rinsed and drained
½ cup (72 g) fresh green peas (if using frozen, thaw first)
1 red onion, chopped
½ tsp turmeric powder
2 tsp (4 g) cumin powder
Juice of 1 lemon
1 cup (16 g) packed cilantro
½ cup (96 g) amaranth
½ cup (46 g) black gram bean flour (urad dal flour)
Salt and pepper to taste
Oil for deep-frying

(continued)

NAAN TACOS *with* GREEN PEA AMARANTH FALAFELS & SPICY AVOCADO CHUTNEY (cont.)

Make the garlic oil for brushing the prepared naan by mixing the minced garlic with the oil. Set aside.

To make the dough for the naan, mix the sugar, 1 tablespoon (15 ml) of water and the yeast in a bowl and set aside to activate for 4 to 5 minutes. In a large bowl mix the flour, salt, oil and the activated yeast mix. Slowly add the water, mixing with your fingers and kneading the dough to bring it together. Knead for a few minutes to form a soft dough that springs back if you press with your finger. Cover with a kitchen towel and leave to rise for 2 to 3 hours.

To make the avocado chutney, in a food processor, puree the avocado, cilantro, mint, coconut yogurt, chili, lemon juice, salt and pepper. Transfer to a bowl and set aside.

For the tahini sauce, mix together the tahini, water, garlic, turmeric, lemon juice and salt. Set aside.

Make the falafel mixture by grinding the chickpeas, green peas, onion, turmeric, cumin, lemon juice, cilantro, amaranth, bean flour, salt and pepper in a food processor until it forms into a smooth paste. Transfer to a bowl and roll the mixture into teaspoon-size balls. Keep aside in a covered bowl until you need to fry them.

Once the naans are closer to being made, heat the oil in a wok until it gets very hot. Lower the heat to medium and fry the falafel balls in small batches for 3 to 4 minutes or until golden brown. Drain on paper towels, cover again and keep aside.

For the naan, knead the risen dough once again for a few minutes. Heat a nonstick pan on high heat and then reduce to medium.

Divide the dough into 6 to 7 portions, or small lemon-size balls. Roll out each ball into a 7-inch (18-cm) circle. Apply a small amount of water to one side of the rolled-out dough. Place the water side down onto the hot pan. Cook for about a minute or until it begins to turn brown. Flip and do the same. Flip a few times until you get a golden brown naan on both sides. Brush with some of the garlic oil, wrap in foil and put aside. Repeat with the rest of the dough balls.

To put together, place some salad greens with cucumber, tomatoes and chopped red onion on each naan and top with 2 to 3 falafels. Drizzle with the turmeric tahini sauce and a spoonful of the avocado chutney. Fold and it's ready to eat.

I have an instant, mouthwatering moment if you say "masoor dal" anywhere near my presence. This dal is to me what chocolate is to some people. Recently a friend visiting from India said my version tasted like the one his mother made. There can, of course, never be a better compliment than that! I have upped this dal's game by adding bitter gourd chips. The bitter gourd keeps true to its name. It is quite bitter, but it is a perfect pairing with this delicious dal. With every mouthful, you get that ever-so-slightly-bitter taste, which is a delightful surprise.

MASOOR DAL *with* BITTER GOURD CHIPS

Serves 4

BITTER GOURD CHIPS
2 cups (300 g) thinly sliced bitter gourd (use frozen if you can't find fresh)

2 tbsp (20 g) rice flour

½ tsp turmeric powder

½ tsp cumin powder

½ tsp salt

2–4 tbsp (30–60 ml) oil

MASOOR DAL
1 tbsp (15 ml) oil

1 medium onion, chopped

2 cloves garlic, sliced

2 green chilies, sliced lengthwise

2 medium tomatoes, chopped

1 cup (192 g) red lentils (split masoor dal), rinsed

4 cups (960 ml) water

TEMPERING
2 tbsp (30 ml) oil

1 tsp cumin

1 medium onion, sliced thin

1 clove garlic

½ tsp red chili powder

For the bitter gourd chips, toss the bitter gourd slices with the rice flour, turmeric, cumin and salt. Leave to rest for at least 30 minutes. The salt will help release the moisture from the bitter gourd.

To make the dal, heat the oil on high heat in a deep pan. Once hot, add the onion and cook until it is translucent, 2 to 3 minutes. Reduce heat to medium and add the garlic and the chilies and then cook for a few minutes or until the raw smell of the garlic has gone. Add the tomatoes and stir while cooking for 3 to 4 minutes until the tomatoes are somewhat mushy. Add the rinsed lentils and stir around for just a few seconds to mix everything together. Add the water and bring to a boil. Lower the heat to low and simmer, covered, for 10 minutes.

Once the bitter gourd has rested, heat the oil in a shallow nonstick pan on high heat. Get the bitter gourd slices ready by brushing off any excess flour and placing them in the pan. Make sure you don't overlap the slices. Give the slices 2 to 3 minutes on each side on high heat. Bitter gourd needs a lot of oil so you may have to replenish the oil in the pan as the slices cook. Turn the slices over once they turn a dark brown color. Transfer to a plate lined with a paper towel and set aside.

Prepare the tempering by heating the oil on high heat. Once hot, add the cumin. When the cumin starts to sputter, after a few seconds, quickly add the onion and garlic. Reduce the heat to medium and cook for 3 to 4 minutes or until the onion begins to brown at the edges. Add the red chili powder and stir continuously while the onion browns further, 1 to 2 minutes. Turn off the heat.

To serve, mix the bitter gourd chips into the dal, reserving some for garnish. Top with the tempering. Garnish with some more bitter gourd chips, cilantro and sliced cucumber on the side.

This dal goes very well with just plain basmati rice.

Mom made *arbi* (taro root) all the time. It was a healthy change from potatoes in our house. Arbi is starchy like potatoes and carries more calories than a potato. It is great for shallow frying, which gives it a lovely toasty taste. Mom also made snake beans a lot. But she never put these two ingredients together. They work really well in partnership—I just adore this combination. It is actually a take on a dish I make often at home, *aloo* (potatoes) beans. I have replaced the potatoes with taro root and the green beans with snake beans.

ARBI & SNAKE BEANS CURRY

Serves 4

ARBI CURRY
1 lb (454 g) taro root (arbi)
Enough water to cook the taro root
1 tbsp (10 g) rice flour
1 tbsp (9 g) coconut flour

2 tbsp (30 ml) oil
Pinch of asafetida
1 tsp mustard seeds
½ tsp turmeric powder
½ tsp chili powder
Salt to taste

SNAKE BEANS
1 tbsp (15 ml) oil
½ tsp carom seeds
1 medium onion, chopped
1 medium tomato, chopped
1 tsp coriander powder
½ tsp red chili powder
½ lb (225 g) snake beans, cut into 2" (5-cm) pieces, blanched for 3–4 minutes
Salt to taste

Place the whole taro root in a deep pan and fill with enough water to cover. Bring the water to a boil and then simmer on low heat for 7 to 8 minutes. Drain and run the root under cold water. Once the root is cool enough to handle, peel off the skin and cut into 1-inch (2.5-cm)-thick circles.

In a shallow pan, mix the rice flour and coconut flour and toss the taro root to cover evenly.

In a nonstick pan, heat the oil on high heat. Once hot, add the asafetida. After only about 30 seconds, add the mustard seeds. After they start to sputter, in a few seconds, add the taro root. Lower the heat to medium-low and after 2 to 3 minutes add the turmeric, chili powder and the salt. Continue to fry the taro root, tossing often so that both sides have the opportunity to get cooked. Fry until the taro root is a golden brown and slightly charred, 10 to 12 minutes. You will also get a lovely crumb from the coconut and rice flour that doesn't stick to the taro root. Transfer the fried roots and the crumbs to a separate bowl when done and set aside.

For the snake beans, in the same pan that you cooked the taro root, heat the oil on high heat. Once hot, add the carom seeds. Once they start to sizzle, in a few seconds, add the onion. Lower the heat to medium and cook the onion until translucent, 3 to 4 minutes. Add the tomato and cook until the tomato is soft and mushy, another 3 to 4 minutes. Add the coriander and chili powder and stir to mix all ingredients. Add the blanched snake beans and stir again to combine the beans with the onion-tomato mix. Cook for around 5 minutes until the beans take on the flavors. Season with salt. Add the taro root and stir to mix in with the snake beans. Serve with a dal and basmati rice.

When I was first introduced to risotto rice many years ago, I turned up my nose to it. I couldn't imagine it being good compared to the mighty basmati. During the years I have warmed up to risotto, and I can tell you that this white lentil risotto can take on the great Arborio rice. In fact I prefer it. And so will you. I chose the white lentil because it is the most naturally creamy lentil—I didn't need to add cheese in this take on risotto. The creamy flavor of this lentil risotto will blow your mind and the slightly sweet, slightly bitter fennel with it is just simply wonderful.

URAD DAL RISOTTO *with* CARAMELIZED FENNEL

Serves 4

RISOTTO
1½ cups (288 g) white lentils (split and dehusked urad dal), soaked overnight

5 cups (1.2 L) vegetable stock

2 tbsp (30 g) coconut oil

2 medium onions, chopped fine

2 cloves garlic, minced

½ tsp Italian seasoning

1 cup (240 ml) white wine

Salt and pepper to taste

CARAMELIZED FENNEL
1 fennel bulb, cut into thin strips, fronds reserved for garnish

2 tsp (10 g) coconut oil

2 tsp (5 g) fennel seeds

Sea salt to taste

1 tbsp (15 ml) maple syrup

Rinse the lentils several times under cold water. Set aside.

Heat the stock in a pan until hot. Lower the heat and let it simmer, keeping it warm for the risotto.

In a deep pot, heat the oil on high heat. Once hot, add the onions and garlic and reduce the heat to low. Stirring often, cook the onions until they are transparent, 3 to 4 minutes. Add the Italian seasoning and give it another stir. Add the lentils and stir to mix everything together. Add the white wine and stir. Simmer and cook until the wine is almost completely absorbed by the lentils. Add 2 cups (480 ml) of stock, making sure that the dal is covered by the stock. Add more if needed.

During the next 30 to 40 minutes, stir the lentils every now and then, checking the level of the stock. Keep adding a little at a time, keeping the lentils wet but not drowned. The cooking time will differ according to how long you soaked the lentils.

For the caramelized fennel, cut the fennel in half and then slice into strips. You will get some pieces that will look like steaks and some just strips. Cook the fennel in batches, making sure that you don't overlap them in the pan. Heat the oil on high heat. Once hot, add the fennel, and make sure each piece is in direct contact with the pan. Without touching the fennel, let it char for a minute or two on each side. Then add the fennel seeds, a sprinkle of sea salt and the maple syrup. Cook on each side again for a few seconds. Keep a close eye on it—after you add the maple syrup the fennel can burn quite quickly. Repeat until all the fennel is cooked and caramelized. Set aside.

Check on the lentils. They should be not mushy but well cooked and should have a tiny bite to them. Season with salt and pepper.

Once done, divide the dal risotto among the bowls and top with the caramelized fennel and the fennel fronds. Drizzle some coconut oil, sprinkle some roasted fennel seeds and serve hot.

Wholesome
SNACKING

Snack time in India is a pretty sacred thing. At a certain time (or times!) in the afternoon, the hustle and bustle will come to a halt and people will stop what they are doing to drink their chai with their scrumptious snacks, sitting around relaxing, not a care in the world. It is the memory of those amazing moments that I have experienced with my mom and my friends that I try to create here with wholesome snacks that are once again merged with Western flavors.

The recipes in this section are perhaps not the classic items to be found on an Indian plate at chai time, but they are my new favorites. Great for a nibble or something heartier where the snack can turn into a meal.

I'm a big fan of hummus just because it is a healthy, perfect accompaniment to so many snacks. I always thought that hummus could only be made with chickpeas but it can really be made with any legume, resulting in a fantastic number of options. These recipes are addictive and sure winners at gatherings.

LENTIL HUMMUS 3 WAYS

Serves 10 to 12

PUY LENTILS & AVOCADO HUMMUS

½ cup (96 g) puy lentils
1 tbsp (6 g) cumin seeds, dry roasted
1 tbsp (15 ml) olive oil
½ avocado
2 tbsp (30 ml) tahini
Juice of ½ lemon
1 clove garlic
½ tsp cumin powder
Sea salt and pepper to taste
½ cup (8 g) fresh cilantro leaves

Rinse the lentils under cold water a few times. Combine the lentils in a pan with water and bring to a boil over high heat. Once the lentils come to a boil, lower the heat to low. Remove any foam with a spoon. Put the lid on and let simmer for around 25 minutes or until the lentils are tender. Take the lentils off the heat once cooked and drain any excess liquid.

In a pan, dry roast the cumin seeds on medium-high heat for a minute.

Add the olive oil and cooked lentils to a food processor along with the avocado, tahini, lemon juice, garlic, cumin, salt and pepper to taste and cilantro. Process for 1 to 2 minutes or until mostly smooth, stopping to scrape down the sides as needed. Don't overprocess, as you want to maintain some texture. Taste and season with more sea salt and black pepper if needed.

Spoon the dip into a serving bowl and garnish with fresh cilantro and roasted cumin seeds. Serve with crackers and fresh veggies.

(continued)

ROASTED RED PEPPER & RED LENTIL HUMMUS

1 red bell pepper, seeded and cut in half

2 tbsp (30 ml) olive oil, divided

Sea salt and pepper to taste

½ cup (96 g) red lentils (split masoor dal)

2 cups (480 ml) water

4 tbsp (60 ml) tahini

Juice of ½ lemon

2 cloves garlic

½ tsp coriander powder

½ tsp cumin powder

½ tsp Kashmiri chili powder

1 tsp piri piri spice

¼ cup (30 g) walnuts

Preheat the oven to 400°F (205°C). Line a baking tray with parchment paper.

Add the red pepper to the baking tray and drizzle with 1 tablespoon (15 ml) of olive oil and lightly season with sea salt and black pepper. Toss to coat.

Roast the pepper in the oven for 15 to 20 minutes until soft.

Rinse the lentils under cold water a few times. Combine the lentils in a pan with water and bring to a boil over high heat. Once the lentils come to a boil, lower the heat to low. Remove any foam with a spoon. Put the lid on and let simmer for around 10 minutes or until the lentils are tender. Take the lentils off the heat and drain.

Add the roasted pepper, remaining 1 tablespoon (15 ml) of olive oil and the cooked lentils to a food processor along with the tahini, lemon juice, garlic, coriander, cumin, Kashmiri chili powder, piri piri spice and salt and pepper to taste. Process for 1 to 2 minutes or until mostly smooth, stopping to scrape down the sides as needed. Add the walnuts and pulse to chop and incorporate. Don't overprocess, as you want to maintain some texture. Taste and season with more salt and pepper, if needed.

Serve garnished with fresh cilantro, walnuts and piri piri spice if desired. Serve with crackers and fresh veggies.

TURMERIC HUMMUS

½ cup (100 g) split chickpeas (chana dal), soaked for 3–4 hours

2 cups (480 ml) water

2 tbsp (30 ml) olive oil

Juice of ½ lemon

1 clove garlic

1 tsp turmeric powder

Salt to taste

Rinse the chickpeas under cold water a few times. Combine them in a pan with the water and bring to a boil over high heat. Once they come to a boil, lower the heat to low. Remove any foam with a spoon. Put the lid on and let simmer for around 25 minutes or until the chickpeas are tender. Take the chickpeas off the heat and drain.

Add the cooked chickpeas to a food processor with the oil, lemon juice, garlic and turmeric. Process for 1 to 2 minutes or until mostly smooth, stopping to scrape down the sides as needed. Don't overprocess, as you want to maintain some texture. Taste and season with salt if needed.

Serve garnished with pumpkin seeds and roasted cumin seeds if desired. Serve with crackers and fresh veggies.

This recipe is based on a savory pancake in India called *chila*. Simple, traditional chilas are made with chickpea flour and almost never have any fillings. It seemed only natural to me to convert the classic chila into a pizza. I wanted to celebrate the greens that I love eating and therefore chose the split green lentils, which even though they are the most used lentils in Holland, they were never made at home in India. You could top this delicious base with any vegetables you love. This makes it a very versatile snack.

SPLIT GREEN PEA PIZZA
with WALNUT MINT CHUTNEY

Serves 4

MINT CHUTNEY
½ cup (45 g) fennel fronds
1 cup (30 g) packed mint
1 green chili
¼ cup (30 g) walnuts
¼ cup (60 ml) olive oil
Salt and pepper to taste

PIZZA CRUST
1 cup (192 g) split green peas, soaked for 4–12 hours
½ cup (120 ml) water
2 cloves garlic
1 tsp cumin powder
1 tsp Italian seasoning
1 green chili
½ tsp baking powder
¼ tsp salt

PIZZA SAUCE
1 tbsp (15 ml) olive oil
1 onion, chopped fine
1 cup (125 g) finely chopped zucchini
1 tbsp (6 g) Italian seasoning
½ tsp fresh or dried sage
1⅔ cups (400 g) canned tomatoes
3 tbsp (45 ml) tomato puree
1 tbsp (15 ml) tomato ketchup
1 tbsp (15 ml) sriracha
Salt and pepper to taste

TOPPINGS
1 tbsp (15 ml) olive oil
1 cup (90 g) broccoli florets
1 cup (60 g) sugar snap peas
1 cup (92 g) sliced green bell pepper
1 cup (135 g) asparagus tips
8–10 cherry tomatoes

1 tsp oil (or oil for spraying on a nonstick pan)

(continued)

SPLIT GREEN PEA PIZZA *with* WALNUT MINT CHUTNEY (cont.)

Preheat the oven to 425°F (218°C) and line a baking tray with parchment paper.

For the mint chutney, process the fennel, mint, green chili, walnuts, oil, salt and pepper together in a food processor. Grind until all the ingredients are crushed. Don't process too much. I like this chutney somewhat chunky.

For the pizza crust, rinse the split green peas. Grind the peas with the water in a food processor until it forms into a thick paste. Add the garlic, cumin, Italian seasoning, chili, baking powder and salt and grind until everything is incorporated into the paste. The paste should be smooth enough that when you rub a little between two fingers, you should not feel too much grain. Transfer to a bowl and cover with a damp kitchen towel.

Heat the oil in a pan on high heat for the pizza sauce. Once hot, add the onion and cook until it is translucent, 3 to 4 minutes. Reduce the heat to medium and add the zucchini, Italian seasoning and sage. Stir and cook for 4 to 5 minutes or until the zucchini is soft. Add the canned tomatoes, tomato puree, tomato ketchup and sriracha. Reduce the heat to medium-low and let simmer for 8 to 10 minutes, stirring every now and then. Right at the end, season with salt and pepper and take off the heat.

In a different pan, heat the oil for the toppings on high heat. When hot, add the broccoli, snap peas, pepper and asparagus and cook for just a few minutes until you see very slight charring. Take off the heat and set aside.

Divide the batter into portions according to how big you want the pizzas. I got 4 crusts of 8 inches (20 cm) each. Spray a flat nonstick pan with oil. Pour out the batter and leave to cook on medium heat for a few minutes until the top of the pancake begins to look cooked. Take care to flip very carefully so as not to break it. Because the batter is freshly made from the lentils, it is very delicate. Once flipped, cook for another few minutes. Transfer to the lined baking tray. Allow the crust to cool slightly. Cover the crust with sauce, leaving ½ inch (13 mm) around the edges. Repeat with the entire batter and sauce.

Add the charred toppings and the cherry tomatoes and pop into the oven for 15 to 18 minutes.

Once done, add the chutney, chili flakes, some dukkah and garnish with some mint. Serve hot!

note: The longer you soak the split peas, the shorter the time needed to grind them in a food processor.

The king of legumes for me is the chickpea. It can literally be eaten with anything, and it tastes like a million bucks. Depending on the amount of cooking, chickpeas can be creamy or crunchy. In this dish they are slightly crunchy to the very crunchy radicchio, offset with the tanginess of the oranges. This is a light, refreshing salad and is a great cleansing meal.

MASALA CHICKPEA SALAD *with* RADICCHIO & ORANGES

Serves 4

RASPBERRY DRESSING
½ cup (60 g) raspberries
1 shallot, chopped very fine
2 tbsp (30 ml) white wine vinegar
1 clove garlic
1 tbsp (13 g) sugar
1 tbsp (15 ml) olive oil
Salt and pepper to taste

SALAD
3⅓ cups (550 g) canned chickpeas
1 cup (260 g) canned white beans
1 tbsp (15 ml) olive oil
1 tsp cumin powder
½ tsp red chili powder
½ tsp ginger powder
½ tsp turmeric powder
½ tsp chana masala
Sea salt and pepper to taste

2 large oranges
1 small head radicchio (use more depending on the size), roughly torn
½ cup (10 g) salad greens
8–10 basil leaves

For the dressing, crush the raspberries and mix in with the shallot, vinegar, garlic, sugar, oil, salt and pepper. Stir well to combine. Set aside.

Preheat the oven to 400°F (205°C). Line a baking tray with parchment paper.

Rinse the chickpeas and the white beans thoroughly but separately. Leave to dry on kitchen towels for about 30 minutes.

Place the chickpeas on the lined tray. Bake for 15 minutes. Transfer to a bowl and mix in the white beans. Add the olive oil, cumin, chili powder, ginger, turmeric, chana masala, salt and pepper and toss to mix in everything.

Spread on the baking sheet and bake for another 10 minutes. Once they are done, turn off the oven and leave the oven door a little open to keep the chickpea mix warm.

Peel the oranges and cut crosswise into circle slices. Cut the radicchio in half, core it and discard any wilted leaves on the outside. Tear the leaves and place them in a deep bowl or large plate. Scoop the chickpea mix onto the radicchio. Place the orange slices randomly on top of the chickpeas and then scatter some salad greens and basil leaves. Drizzle the raspberry dressing and add some extra sea salt and pepper. Sprinkle with chana masala to finish off the salad.

Vegetables make healthy snacks for in-between meals. They are my favorite, and you don't have to be boring by just eating them raw. My mother used to make us pakodas every time we sat to watch a movie together at home. This recipe is my take on a pakoda, made very differently. This version is much healthier than the deep-fried version. It is an addictive snack along with the bursting-with-flavor tomato chutney, which is terribly versatile and can be eaten with any curry on the side or as a salsa with just some tortilla chips too.

TIKKA MASALA CAULIFLOWER BITES
with ROASTED TOMATO CHUTNEY

Serves 4 to 6

ROASTED TOMATO CHUTNEY

2 big tomatoes, cut in half

½ red bell pepper, seeded

3 tbsp (45 ml) oil, divided

1 red onion, chopped fine

1 tsp nigella seeds (kalonji)

¼ tsp fenugreek seeds

1 clove garlic, minced

1 red chili, chopped fine (add more if you like the chutney spicier)

1 tbsp (15 ml) white wine vinegar

2 tbsp (28 g) jaggery

1 tsp Dijon mustard

Salt to taste

TIKKA MASALA CAULIFLOWER

2 cloves garlic, minced

1" (2.5-cm) piece ginger, grated

1½ tsp (4 g) turmeric powder

½ tsp red chili powder

1 tsp coriander powder

2 tbsp (11 g) chickpea flour (besan)

Salt to taste

1 cup (240 ml) coconut milk

1 lb (454 g) cauliflower, cut into bite-size florets

Preheat the oven to 425°F (218°C). Line a baking tray with parchment paper.

For the roasted tomato chutney, place the tomatoes and bell pepper cut side up on the lined tray. Drizzle with 1 tablespoon (15 ml) of oil and bake for 20 minutes. Remove from the oven and let cool. Heat 2 tablespoons (30 ml) of oil in a pan. Once hot, add the onion, nigella and fenugreek seeds, garlic and red chili. Cook for 2 to 3 minutes, reduce the heat to medium-low and then add the roasted tomatoes and bell pepper. With your spoon, crush the tomatoes and bell pepper while stirring. Continue to cook for another 2 to 3 minutes. Add the vinegar and jaggery and stir until the jaggery has dissolved into the tomato mix, about a minute. Add the mustard, lower the heat to low and simmer for 5 to 8 minutes. Season with salt, take off the heat and let cool.

Reduce the oven temperature to 395°F (202°C). Line a baking tray with parchment paper.

In a bowl, mix the garlic, ginger, turmeric, chili, coriander, flour and salt into the coconut milk. Toss the cauliflower florets into this spice mix, making sure you cover all sides completely. Bake the cauliflower on the lined tray for 35 to 40 minutes. Turn over the cauliflower halfway through.

Garnish with cilantro and serve hot with the tomato chutney.

My mom's favorite snack is *namkeen*, which very often is made with deep-fried legumes, lentils and other elements. Namkeen is a savory snack-lovers delight, and there is always a fair assortment of namkeen at any home in India. Like a true Indian, my daughter loves namkeen. Her most beloved namkeen is moong dal. Even though I had never thought of making it at home, this is a very simple snack to prepare and is satisfying to munch on. You could use almost any legume to make this snack, only the time to fry it may differ a bit.

CRUNCHY LENTILS

Serves 6 to 8

½ cup (108 g) split and dehusked mung beans (moong dal), soaked for 1 hour

½ cup (100 g) split chickpeas (chana dal), soaked for 1 hour

½ cup (96 g) brown lentils (whole masoor dal), soaked for 1 hour

½ cup (96 g) red lentils (split masoor dal), soaked for 1 hour

Oil for deep-frying

Salt and pepper to taste

1 onion, diced small

Soak the beans, chickpeas and lentils separately. After an hour, rinse and wash thoroughly.

Place each legume separately on some kitchen towels to dry. Let dry for at least 1 hour.

Heat enough oil in a wok for deep-frying. Once very hot, fry each legume and lentil separately while stirring constantly.

- For the split mung beans, 2 to 3 minutes.

- For the chickpeas, 3 to 4 minutes.

- For the whole brown lentils, just a few seconds.

- For the red lentils, 2 to 3 minutes.

When done frying, season to taste with salt and pepper. Transfer the fried beans, chickpeas and lentils with a slotted spoon from the oil to a bowl lined with kitchen towels. Let them completely cool down. They will stay good in an airtight container for up to a week.

Just before serving, add the onion and pomegranate arils. The onion and the pomegranate will make the lentils soggy, so do not store with the garnish mixed in.

My memories of chilas, Indian pancakes, are clear as day. I remember Mom rushing into the kitchen to prepare some for whenever my dad felt hungry in the late afternoons. My mother's chilas were always made with chickpea flour, an Indian pantry staple, and super easy and simple to make. A quick snack, where you throw everything together in a bowl, add some water and voila, you have a filling snack that is super healthy too. I have changed my mom's version with mung bean flours and added some additional elements that make it even more exciting for me.

MOONG DAL CHIVE CHILAS

Serves 4 to 6

GINGER SOY DIPPING SAUCE
2 tbsp (30 ml) soy sauce

1 tbsp (15 ml) rice vinegar

1 tbsp (15 ml) water

1 tsp sesame oil

1 tsp sugar

½" (13-mm) piece ginger, grated

2 tbsp (18 g) sesame seeds, toasted

MOONG BEAN CHIVES CHILAS
1 cup (92 g) split mung bean flour (moong dal flour)

½ cup (46 g) black mung bean flour (whole moong dal flour)

1 small onion, chopped fine

1 red chili, chopped fine

½ tsp turmeric powder

¼ tsp carom seeds

1 tbsp (15 ml) miso paste

¼ cup (15 g) chives, chopped into 3–4 parts

¼ cup (4 g) cilantro, tightly packed, chopped roughly

1 cup (240 ml) water

1–2 tbsp (15–30 ml) oil

For the dipping sauce, combine the soy sauce, vinegar, water, oil, sugar, ginger and sesame seeds and set aside.

Sieve and mix together the split and black mung bean flours. Mix together with the onion, chili, turmeric, carom, miso, chives and cilantro. Add the water. The batter should resemble pancake batter. If the batter is too thick you may need more water. Add a tablespoon or two (15 to 30 ml) at a time to make it thinner.

Heat a teaspoon of oil at a time on high heat in a nonstick pan. Once hot, lower the heat to medium and add enough batter to cover the bottom of the pan. Use the back of the ladle to spread the mix. Let the chila cook for a minute or two. Flip when you see the edges brown a little and the top begins to look cooked. Be gentle while flipping. Cook the other side for a few minutes and then transfer to a plate lined with a paper towel. Repeat with all the batter.

Chilas should always be served hot. Eat by dipping into the ginger soy sauce.

note: *If you can't find mung bean flour you can make it from scratch. For moong dal, soak for 1 hour. For urad dal, soak for 4 to 8 hours. Rinse, drain and grind them in a food processor until a thick paste forms. The paste should be smooth enough that when you rub between two fingers, you should not feel too much grain. Follow the recipe same as above.*

A pakoda in India is anything that is first coated with a lentil batter and then deep-fried. This particular pakoda snack has its roots in my childhood. It is a very popular street snack too if you want something filling on the go. I remember treating myself to it, once in a blue moon, if I had money at school to buy it. It can be made with any kind of bread and has layers of deliciousness locked in. Bread pakodas are also an extremely comforting snack, very filling and perfect as a snack for watching a good movie.

BLACK BEAN & POTATO CURRY STUFFED IN BREAD PAKODAS

Serves 6 to 8

APRICOT TAMARIND CHUTNEY
½ cup (120 ml) water
½ cup (60 g) dried apricots, cut roughly into chunks
½ cup (70 g) dates, sliced
4 tbsp (60 ml) tamarind pulp
1 tbsp (15 ml) date syrup
2 tbsp (28 g) jaggery
½ tsp chili powder
½ tsp cumin powder

CILANTRO CHUTNEY
1 cup (16 g) tightly packed cilantro
½ cup (15 g) tightly packed mint
1 green or red chili (add more or less according to taste)
1 clove garlic
1 tsp lime juice
1 tsp sugar
1 tbsp (15 ml) olive oil
Salt to taste

CHICKPEA BATTER
1 cup (92 g) chickpea flour (besan)
½ cup (120 ml) water
½ tsp turmeric powder
½ tsp red chili powder
½ tsp baking powder
Salt to taste

BREAD PAKODA FILLING
1 tbsp (15 ml) oil
1 tsp mustard seeds
4–5 curry leaves
2 medium potatoes, boiled and mashed
½ cup (108 g) canned black beans, rinsed
¼ tsp turmeric powder
Salt to taste

Oil for deep-frying
8 slices of white bread (I prefer the bread be at least 1–2 days old. Too fresh and it will fall apart.)
1 red onion, chopped fine
½ cup (8 g) cilantro, chopped fine

(continued)

BLACK BEAN & POTATO CURRY STUFFED IN BREAD PAKODAS (cont.)

To make the apricot tamarind chutney, combine the water, apricots and dates in a pan. Simmer on low heat for 10 to 12 minutes or until the apricots and dates are soft. Turn off the heat, transfer to a food processor and grind to a fine paste. Once done, run through a sieve and transfer to the pan you cooked it in. On low heat add the tamarind pulp, date syrup, jaggery, chili powder and cumin and stir to give it a good mix. Cook for a few minutes and then transfer to a bowl. Let cool.

For the cilantro chutney, combine the cilantro, mint, chili, garlic, lime juice, sugar, oil and salt in a food processor and blitz to a fine sauce. Transfer to a bowl and set aside.

For the chickpea batter, combine the chickpea flour, water, turmeric, chili powder, baking powder and salt in a flat, shallow bowl. Mix well and set aside.

For the filling, heat the oil in a pan on high heat. Once hot, add the mustard seeds. Once they start to sputter, after a few seconds, lower the heat to medium and add the curry leaves and cook for 30 seconds. Add the potatoes, beans, turmeric and salt. Cook for around 5 minutes, stirring to mix all the ingredients. Take off the heat and set aside.

Heat enough oil in a shallow pan for deep-frying.

To assemble the pakodas, place a slice of bread on a cutting board. Spread a thin layer of the cilantro chutney, then a layer of the potato-and-bean filling. Sprinkle some chopped red onion and cilantro on top. Place another slice of bread on top of the first one. Cut in half diagonally and press down slightly to seal. Repeat with all the slices of bread.

Dip each triangle sandwich into the chickpea batter, coating evenly on all sides and letting any excess drip off.

Once the oil is hot, reduce the heat to medium. Fry one or two triangle sandwiches at a time for a few minutes on each side while flipping them every now and then. Remove from the oil with a slotted spoon and transfer to a bowl lined with kitchen towels. Repeat with all the bread triangles.

Serve hot with any excess cilantro chutney and apricot date chutney for dipping.

note: *Pakodas should always be eaten hot, as they tend to go soggy after a while.*

Pav in Hindi means bread buns and *bhaji* a thick curry with vegetables. It is famous in Mumbai, and two years ago I tasted the most delicious kind when I visited the city for a project. It was a modest restaurant, with people lining up for hours just to sit and enjoy this spicy treat. I haven't forgotten that experience and since then have longed to re-create it in my own kitchen. My version makes it a burger and combines it with a spicy mango chutney. The result was so good and the burger patties kept so well that I have been eating it every day for days.

PAV BHAJI BURGERS *with* SPICY MANGO CHUTNEY

Serves 6 to 8

MANGO CHUTNEY
1 tbsp (15 ml) oil
¼ tsp mustard seeds
¼ tsp fenugreek seeds
¼ tsp whole peppercorns
½ tsp nigella seeds (kalonji)
½ tsp fennel seeds
4 whole cloves
Pinch of asafetida
1 unripe mango, seeded and cut into thin strips
½" (13-mm) piece ginger, grated
½ tsp turmeric powder
½ tsp cumin powder
1 tsp red chili powder
1 tbsp (15 ml) white wine vinegar
¼ cup (60 ml) water
2–3 tbsp (28–42 g) jaggery
Salt to taste

PAV BHAJI SPICE MIX
1 black cardamom pod
2 tbsp (10 g) coriander seeds
1 tbsp (6 g) cumin seeds
1 tsp peppercorns
¼ tsp fennel seeds
1 dried red chili
3 whole cloves
½ tbsp (6 g) dry mango powder (amchoor)

PAV BHAJI BURGERS PATTY
18 oz (510 g) boiled potatoes
4 oz (112 g) cooked carrots
1 cup (150 g) broad beans (fava beans)
1 red onion
1 clove garlic
2 tbsp (13 g) broken flax seeds
1 tsp red chili powder
½ cup (54 g) bread crumbs
Salt to taste
5 tsp (25 g) coconut oil, divided

8 soft bread buns, sliced in half

(continued)

PAV BHAJI BURGERS *with* SPICY MANGO CHUTNEY
(cont.)

For the mango chutney, heat the oil in a pan on high heat and add the mustard, fenugreek, peppercorns, nigella, fennel, cloves and a pinch of asafetida. Once the seeds begin to sputter, after a few seconds, lower the heat to medium and add the mango strips and the ginger. Stir to mix and add the turmeric, cumin, red chili, vinegar, water and jaggery. Lower the heat to low, add the salt and let simmer for 10 to 15 minutes until the mango is completely soft and cooked. Once done, set aside to cool.

For the pav bhaji spice mix, dry roast the cardamom, coriander, cumin, peppercorns, fennel, chili and cloves for about a minute on low heat until the spices are fragrant. Transfer to a spice grinder and grind to a fine powder. Add in the dry mango powder. Store any leftover spice for several weeks in an airtight container.

For the patty, add the potatoes, carrots, beans, onion, garlic, flax, chili powder, bread crumbs, salt, 3 teaspoons (15 ml) of oil and 3 teaspoons (6 g) of spice mix to a food processor and mix until everything is broken down and well combined.

Form about a half a cup (120 g) at a time in the palm of your hands into 6 to 8 patties.

Melt 1 teaspoon of coconut oil at a time on medium heat and fry the patties in batches. Cook each side for 2 to 3 minutes or until golden brown. Repeat with the rest of the patties.

Heat 1 teaspoon of coconut oil in a griddle on high heat. Once hot, grill the buns, cut side down, for a minute on each side.

To build the burger, place one patty on each bottom bun. Smear with 1 tablespoon (15 ml) of the mango chutney, top with baby spinach leaves, red onion slices, tomato slices, cucumber ribbons and some cilantro. Drizzle with tomato ketchup and cover with the top bun.

There are a lot of ingredients that I wasn't exposed to in India where I grew up, and collard greens is one of them. Collard greens, or haakh as they are called in the Kashmir region, form a vital part of their meals. Even though the Kashmiri people never really use this leaf in its raw form, in the West it is not uncommon to do so. I have paired the leaves with some yummy lentils, grain and vegetables. It is quick to make and quite delicious. The leaves are delightfully crunchy with the other raw ingredients and the spicy tahini sauce adds creamy heat.

HAAKH LEAF LENTIL WRAPS *with* SRIRACHA TAHINI SAUCE

Serves 6 to 8

SPICY TAHINI SAUCE
½ cup (120 ml) tahini
2 tsp (10 ml) soy sauce
1 tbsp (15 ml) sriracha sauce
1 tbsp (15 ml) maple syrup
Juice of 1 lime
1 tbsp (6 g) grated ginger
1 tbsp (15 ml) water

LENTIL WRAPS
1 tbsp (15 ml) oil
½ tsp cumin seeds
1 cup (240 g) canned brown lentils (whole masoor dal)
Salt to taste

½ cup (100 g) cooked spelt grain
1 cup (125 g) sliced strips zucchini
1 cup (92 g) sliced strips green bell pepper
1 cup (125 g) sliced strips carrots
1 cup (130 g) sliced strips cucumber
1 cup (30 g) baby spinach leaves
6–8 collard greens, stems trimmed off

For the tahini sauce, whisk together the tahini, soy sauce, sriracha, maple syrup, lime juice, ginger and water and set aside.

For the lentil wraps, heat the oil in a pan on high heat. Once hot, add the cumin seeds. Once they start to sputter, after a few seconds, lower the heat to medium and add the lentils. Cook while stirring for a few minutes. Add the salt and set aside to cool.

Divide the spelt grain, zucchini, bell pepper, carrots, cucumber and spinach into 6 or 7 portions.

Lay one leaf on a cutting board and layer the ingredients one by one on the center of the leaf. Fold the bottom in and then the sides to seal the wrap like a burrito. Cut in half. I used a cocktail prick to hold the leaves together.

Dip the wrap into the tahini sauce or pour with a spoon on the wrap and bite in.

This recipe is my way of bringing New Delhi and Rotterdam together. This recipe is based on very popular street snacks from both cities. The idea behind both favorites is to put together all of what you could want in a decadent street snack, all on one plate. It has fries, salad, curry sauces and lentil fritters. At first look, all ingredients seem unlikely companions, but when you taste them together, you will keep coming back for more.

SHAWARMA SWEET POTATO & CELERIAC FRIES with URAD DAL FRITTERS, CURRY PEANUT SAUCE & PARSLEY CHUTNEY

Serves 4 to 6

SWEET POTATO AND CELERIAC FRIES
12 oz (340 g) sweet potato, cut ¼" (6-mm)-thick strips
10 oz (280 g) celeriac root, cut into ¼" (6-mm)-thick strips
2 tbsp (30 ml) olive oil
½ tsp cinnamon
3 crushed cloves
2 tsp (5 g) coriander powder
½ tsp ginger powder
2 tsp (5 g) paprika powder
1 tbsp (6 g) cumin seeds
½ tsp black pepper powder
1 tsp fennel seeds
Salt to taste

PARSLEY CHUTNEY
1½ cups (90 g) parsley
2 tsp (8 g) sugar
1 red chili
¼ cup (60 ml) olive oil
1 clove garlic
1 tsp lemon juice
Salt to taste

CURRY PEANUT SAUCE
1 tbsp (15 ml) oil
½ onion, chopped fine
1 clove garlic, minced

2 heaped tbsp (12 g) desiccated coconut
½ cup (120 ml) water
½ cup (120 ml) coconut milk
3 tbsp (45 ml) peanut butter
2 tbsp (30 ml) kecap manis or 1½ tbsp (22 ml) soy sauce
1 tsp brown sugar
1 tsp sambal (or any other chili sauce)
2 tsp (5 g) curry powder
Juice of ½ lemon

URAD DAL FRITTERS
¾ cup (144 g) white lentils (split and dehusked urad dal), soaked overnight
¼ cup (50 g) split chickpeas (chana dal), soaked overnight
½ tsp baking powder
1" (2.5-cm) piece ginger
1 green chili
1 tsp cumin seeds
Pinch of asafetida
Salt to taste
Oil for deep-frying
2 cups (80 g) shredded salad
2 cups (140 g) shredded red cabbage

(continued)

SHAWARMA SWEET POTATO & CELERIAC FRIES with **URAD DAL FRITTERS, CURRY PEANUT SAUCE & PARSLEY CHUTNEY** (cont.)

Preheat the oven to 450°F (232°C). Line a baking tray with parchment paper.

For the fries, toss the sweet potato and celeriac strips with the oil, cinnamon, cloves, coriander, ginger, paprika, cumin, pepper, fennel and salt. I usually just use a big resealable bag and add all the elements and then shake to combine. Transfer to the lined baking tray. Do not overlap the fries. Bake for 25 to 30 minutes.

Make the chutney by grinding the parsley, sugar, chili, oil, garlic, lemon juice and salt in a food processor to a smooth paste. Transfer to a bowl and set aside.

Make the peanut sauce by heating the oil in a pan on high heat. Once hot, add the onion, garlic and coconut. Cook for a few minutes or until the coconut begins to brown a little, about 2 minutes. Add the water and then the coconut milk, lower the heat to medium and add the peanut butter. Stir to mix in the peanut butter. Once the peanut butter is fully mixed in, lower the heat to low and add the kecap manis, sugar, sambal and curry powder. Cook while stirring for 4 to 5 minutes. Add the lemon juice, mix in and cook for another 2 to 3 minutes. Take off the heat and set aside to cool.

For the fritters, rinse the lentils and split chickpeas and then combine in a food processor with the baking powder, ginger, chili, cumin, asafetida and salt. Grind to a smooth paste. Heat enough oil in a wok to deep-fry the fritters. You can test if the oil is hot enough by dropping in a tiny bit of the batter. If it sizzles and rises up, the oil is ready. Fry the fritters in batches by taking a heaped teaspoon at a time, roughly forming into a ball and dropping carefully into the hot oil. Use up all the batter. Remove with a slotted spoon and transfer to a bowl lined with kitchen towels.

To serve, put a handful of shredded salad on a plate. Top with the fries, then with some more shredded salad and shredded red cabbage. Break 3 to 4 fritters in two and scatter on the plate. Top with some grated daikon radish, cherry tomatoes, parsley chutney and peanut sauce.

I am an army kid and one of the most popular items on the menu at any army mess hall was always the cutlet. They were always made with potato and were delicious. I remember plate in hand, topped with cutlets and a generous helping of tomato ketchup, heading to the mess library, sitting down and eating the cutlets in delight with my favorite comics. Sweet memories.

My version of the cutlet is slightly different. Although it doesn't ignore the potato, it has an addition of my favorite bean, the borlotti, and pearl tapioca, which is the prettiest of ingredients. It resulted in a beautiful cutlet, which if you like could also be used as a patty in a burger!

PEARL TAPIOCA & RAJMA BEAN CUTLET with POMEGRANATE MINT CHUTNEY

Serves 6 to 8

POMEGRANATE MINT CHUTNEY
1 cup (30 g) tightly packed mint
¼ cup (4 g) cilantro
1 green chili
½ tsp sugar
⅓ cup (60 g) pomegranate arils
Juice of ½ lemon
¼ tsp black salt
¼ cup (60 ml) water

PEARL TAPIOCA & RAJMA BEAN CUTLET
1 cup (208 g) borlotti beans, soaked overnight
3 cups (720 ml) water
1 medium potato, boiled
½ cup (76 g) pearl tapioca, soaked overnight

1 tsp raisins, chopped
1 green chili, chopped
1" (2.5-cm) piece ginger, grated
1 medium onion, chopped fine
½ tsp cumin powder
½ tsp mango powder (amchoor)
½ tsp turmeric powder
¼ cup (27 g) bread crumbs
Salt and pepper to taste
1–2 tbsp (15–30 ml) oil

(continued)

PEARL TAPIOCA & RAJMA BEAN CUTLET
with POMEGRANATE MINT CHUTNEY (cont.)

For the chutney, grind the mint, cilantro, chili, sugar, pomegranate, lemon juice, salt and water in a food processor to a fine paste. Set aside.

Drain and rinse the beans a few times under cold water. If using a pressure cooker, combine the beans with the water and give 3 whistles on high heat. Lower the heat to low and cook for 20 minutes. If not using a pressure cooker, cook the beans with the same amount of water. Bring to a boil, then lower the heat and cook, covered, for 50 to 60 minutes or until the beans are very soft and easy to mash.

Drain the beans and transfer to a big bowl. Mash the beans along with the boiled potato.

Drain and rinse the tapioca and add to the mashed beans and potato. Add the raisins, chili, ginger, onion, cumin, mango powder, turmeric, bread crumbs, salt and pepper. Mix and combine all the ingredients with your hands. Take half a cup (120 g) at a time to form the mixture into cutlets. You should have 8 or 9 discs.

Heat a teaspoon of oil at a time in a nonstick pan on high heat. Once hot, lower the heat to medium low and cook 2 or 3 cutlets at a time. Cook for 5 to 6 minutes on each side. Repeat with the rest of the cutlets.

Serve by garnishing with pomegranate arils and cilantro with the pomegranate chutney on the side as a dip.

Bhelpuri is a popular savory snack in India often served on the streets and beaches of Mumbai. It usually has puffed rice (among other ingredients), which I replace here with sprouted moong dal. It has spicy tamarind chutney mixed in to give it that lovely tangy flavor. I have replaced the chutney with the mango vinaigrette to great success. This is a very refreshing snack, and can be substituted as a nutritious meal if you are looking for something light.

SPROUTED MOONG DAL BHELPURI *with* MANGO

Serves 6 to 8

BHELPURI
2 cups (415 g) sprouted whole mung beans (whole moong dal)

1 medium onion, chopped fine

1 medium tomato, chopped fine

1–2 green chilies, chopped fine

1 ripe mango, cut in small cubes, reserve 3 tbsp (30 g) for vinaigrette

1 cup (16 g) packed cilantro, chopped fine

2 tsp (10 ml) lemon juice

Salt to taste

MANGO VINAIGRETTE
1 clove garlic

1 tbsp (15 ml) white wine vinegar

1 tsp honey

1 tbsp (15 ml) olive oil

Salt to taste

Rinse the sprouted beans well under cold water and drain them well.

Combine the sprouts with the onion, tomato, chilies, mango, cilantro, lemon juice and salt.

Prepare the mango vinaigrette by combining the reserved mango, garlic, vinegar, honey, oil and salt. Drizzle the mango vinaigrette over the bhelpuri. It is delicious eaten by itself or with some plain nacho chips.

note: *To sprout the beans, soak overnight. In the morning, rinse a few times under cold water and then transfer to a muslin cloth large enough to hold the beans. Place the cloth and beans in a bowl and fold the muslin over the beans to cover. The next day, rinse with cold water again and repeat the process. If the weather is warm, the lentils should sprout within 2 days. The process could take longer in the winter. Try putting the soaked lentils in a warm spot such as the oven.*

ACKNOWLEDGMENTS

I am so grateful for my rich heritage. This book is the result of that culture and history that lives within me. It is that ever-changing Indian in me, the chameleon that can be traditional as well as bohemian, that has allowed me to jump out of conventions to find liberation in a new collaboration of flavors—a combination of flavors of the world merged with my own.

To my mom and dad, who quietly gave up years of their life so I could build mine. To my mom, who taught me that if you work hard, anything is possible. Who instilled a fierce sense of self in me that has made me who I am today. Her simple style of cooking is the very essence of Indian home cooking. Even years after leaving her nest, I look back and try to re-create that safe comfort in food and flavors that are reminiscent of the fragrances in her kitchen. To my sister, Rachna, who is the backbone of the family and provides me with the amazing support structure that only a loving sister could.

To Michiel and Charlize, who happily volunteered to be my guinea pigs for months of testing and for patiently giving me the space to figure it out—on some days just simply helping eat tons of food. To my best friend Charlize who is my biggest fan and critic, grading each dish delightfully and honestly. Her honesty and innocence is what gets me through, every day. Also, for modeling for the book, uncomplainingly and with beautiful grace.

To Axel, for believing in me no matter what and for being there to listen to my mad ideas, always with encouragement and without judgment. For helping me at every stage and for just being there.

To Akshat, whose words, "Just do the work" have stayed with me for every time I have wanted to give up. To Amit, who at the lowest point in my creative life told me to do the hardest thing of all, to let go. Best advice ever.

To my dear friends Jasleen and Ruchi, whose support during the years has been invaluable. Jasleen, for providing me with an extra set of eyes for the manuscript and Ruchi for our intense spiritual conversations.

To Page Street Publishing, for seeing the potential in me to do this book. To the amazing team, Sarah Burke, Marissa Giambelluca, Meg Palmer and Meg Baskis: I will be eternally grateful for your support.

To HK Living, Netherlands, for being so kind as to provide me with some of the props you see in this book that make the pictures come alive.

And last, but certainly not least, to the scores of people on social media who support me on a daily basis. Who are nothing but kind and generous to me. This book is most of all for you.

ABOUT THE AUTHOR

Rakhee Yadav is a food blogger living in The Netherlands for the past 15 years. Her blog uses local produce to create fusion as well as authentic Indian dishes. Originally from India, she is always looking to create recipes that are innovative and aesthetically appealing and believes in food bringing people together. The act of creating and eating food is a true feast for her senses. She is known for her unique style and her dark, moody pictures. Food and photography are a passion that come together on her blog boxofspice. Her blog combines her skills as a graphic artist, food stylist, recipe developer and photographer. She has been covered by various successful online and offline brands such as *Redbook* magazine, *Buzzfeed*, *ThriveMags* and *Where Women Cook*. She was named as one of the top women under "Women that inspire" in *Good Housekeeping India*.

INDEX